Vegetables and Fruit in Pots

ROYAL HORTICULTURAL SOCIETY

Vegetables and Fruit in Pots

Jo Whittingham

LONDON, NEW YORK, MUNICH, MELBOURNE, DELHI

PROJECT EDITOR Zia Allaway
PROJECT ART EDITOR Vicky Read
MANAGING EDITOR Penny Warren
MANAGING ART EDITOR Alison Donovan
PICTURE RESEARCH Lucy Claxton, Susie Peachey
PRODUCTION EDITOR Andy Hilliard

RHS PUBLISHER Rae Spencer-Jones
RHS EDITOR Simon Maughan

PHOTOGRAPHY Peter Anderson, Brian North

First published in Great Britain in 2012 by
Dorling Kindersley Ltd
Penguin Books Ltd
80 Strand
London WC2R 0RL

2 4 6 8 10 9 7 5 3 1

001–181832–Feb/2012

A CIP catalogue record for this book is available
from the British Library.

ISBN 978-1-4053-7675-4

Printed and bound by Star Standard Industries Pte Ltd, Singapore

To find out more about RHS membership, contact:
RHS Membership Department
PO Box 313, London SW1P 2PE
Telephone: 0845 062 1111
www.rhs.org.uk

Discover more at
www.dk.com

Contents

Jo Whittingham is an author and gardening
journalist, specializing in fruit and vegetables. Her
book titles include *Vegetables in a Small Garden*
in the RHS Simple Steps series, and she also writes
a monthly column for *The Scotsman* newspaper.

Edible inspirations

Pots provide space to grow bumper crops of fruit, vegetables, and herbs, whatever your garden size or style. They also offer the opportunity to decorate your plot with stunning displays to rival any flower garden. Take advantage of productive plants' lush foliage, beautiful blossom, jewel-like fruit, and fascinating roots and pods, and inject more colour into the mix with some edible flowers, like violas, nasturtiums, and the pompons of chives. The containers themselves can also add a decorative touch, flattering each crop and lending your growing space a unique style. This chapter is brimming with ideas to help you develop a productive container garden that will provide a feast for both your eyes and your plate.

Productive pots for patios

Infuse a sunny patio with colour, texture, and rich pickings by planting a range of crops in stylish pots. Devise creative ways to use all the available space, and grow fruit and vegetables that can be cooked or eaten fresh from the plant.

Captions clockwise from left

Pack your patio with a feast of productive plants. Valuable vertical space is often overlooked, but training plants, such as a blackberry, up fences and walls allows them to grow to their full size without invading your outdoor space. The diversity of edibles on this deck guarantees year-round picking too. Mixed loose-leaf lettuces look great springing from containers next to trailing nasturtiums and are ready to cut just six weeks after sowing. Try sowing seed every two or three weeks for salad leaves from spring to autumn. Celeriac will not mature until autumn, but its large parsley-like foliage looks impressive as it grows. For winter interest, include evergreen herbs, such as aromatic rosemary, and hardy vegetables, like kale, both of which can be picked sparingly through the colder months.

Citrus trees enjoy a sunny spot and bring a Mediterranean flavour to a summer patio. Growing citrus in containers is recommended because it allows you to move these tender plants indoors when autumn arrives and return them to the patio in late spring after the last frosts. Other fruit trees, including peaches, apricots, and figs, also need a sunny situation, but are hardy enough to stay outside all year.

Perching pots on a ladder in a small space maximizes the potential for growing all kinds of fruit, vegetables, and herbs. This quirky combination makes use of rustic terracotta pots and recycled cans to grow parsley, thyme, dwarf chillies, and violas, but many other crop plants would work equally well. Try trailing cherry tomatoes, strawberries, and salad leaves, or allow climbing beans, cucumbers, or squashes to scramble up the ladder from large containers set at the base. Pots of trailing plants may need securing to the ladder to prevent them toppling over and climbing plants will need tying in to keep them on the right track.

Productive pots for the garden

Containers can be used to add structure and style to your garden, as well as offering extra space for crops. Where existing soil conditions are poor, pots can also provide the right growing conditions.

Captions clockwise from left

Fruit trees flourish in large pots and introduce valuable height into a small plot. Here, a row of tall peach trees, underplanted with a frill of lettuces, creates an attractive screen and provides dappled shade in summer, as well as delicious fruits. Many fruit trees make ornamental container features with their beautiful spring blossom and branches laden with ripe delicacies. You can also train the stems against walls and fences to take full advantage of the vertical space in the garden. Regular watering and feeding is essential for trees to crop well in containers.

Fixing pots to a pergola is just one way of squeezing more productive plants into the garden. Strawberries are perfect for growing in elevated positions, where their clusters of scarlet berries will hang enticingly over the edge of the pot, making them easy to pick, but more difficult for slugs and birds to reach than berries on the ground. Small containers dry out quickly, so make watering them a daily priority.

Crops set within a flower border provide a focal point while their colours and forms complement the adjacent ornamental plants. Silvery-blue kohl rabi leaves and bright variegated mint stand out against the deep green foliage of celeriac and surrounding shrubs in this arrangement. Scattering pots of fruit and vegetables in sunny spots between flowers can also make it more difficult for pests to locate them, and helps to attract pollinating insects where they are required for a good crop.

Add glamour to a small garden with large, modern galvanized tanks packed with a colourful array of leafy crops, herbs, and climbing beans clambering up stylish metal spirals. The waist-high planting also brings the eye up and can make a small garden feel larger, while spacious planters provide generous growing areas that are easier to maintain than little pots, since they retain more water. Soften the metal's angular lines with drifts of herbs planted at the base; here, the purple pompon flowers of chives flatter the silvery-grey galvanized steel.

Compact crops for tiny spaces

Containers brimming with vegetables, fruits, and herbs can supply colour and convenient crops in a sunny space on a terrace, balcony, or windowsill. Just ensure that pots are secured carefully.

Captions clockwise from top left

Deep window boxes are ideal for apartments, providing high-rise growing spaces that are both practical and productive. Choose large containers, like this substantial metal box, to provide space for crops, such as trailing cherry tomatoes and chilli plants, and a selection of complementary flowers. These plants all prefer full sun, but the drying effects of the heat and wind mean they will need watering at least once a day in summer.

Green wall systems are the ultimate space-saving crop containers and create a lush, vertical tapestry of foliage and fruits. Specially designed fabric pockets are firmly attached to a framework on the wall, which you then fill with compost and plant up. The plants can be either watered and fed by hand or you can install an irrigation system to do the job for you.

Create a decorative screen perfect for terraces and balconies with a row of towering sweetcorn plants. Grow this elegant fruiting vegetable in groups for good pollination, and plant in large, deep pots to provide a delicious crop of cobs.

Plant soft fruit on a balcony in large stylish pots and choose a selection of berries and currants that will provide a long harvest throughout summer and autumn. These vigorous plants make attractive specimens, and are also useful for providing privacy or just a verdant space to relax. Blackcurrants, redcurrants, and blueberries are good choices, while the scrambling stems of thornless blackberry cultivars look great trained on trellis or railings.

Rustic wooden window boxes are simple to make, and you can tailor them to fit your window ledge exactly. Line them with plastic, pierced at the base to provide drainage, and fill with a cottage-garden-inspired display of flowering herbs and salad leaves. Compact, purple-flowered thyme, glowing golden marjoram and lofty tarragon make good planting partners for a sunny sill. A strip of copper around the container adds a decorative flourish and will also deter adventurous slugs and snails.

Mini allotments in raised beds

Raised beds are easy to construct and maintain, and allow you to pack a huge range of crops into a limited space. Make room for your own mini allotment on any sunny patio or terrace.

Captions clockwise from top left

Deep raised beds built from sturdy timber have an appealing rustic style and provide the perfect home for a wide variety of crops. They hold a good depth of compost and retain moisture well, which allows dense planting and suits hungry crops, like the cherry plum tomatoes shown here. The compost warms up quickly, too, giving heat-loving basil and other tender crops a boost. Root crops also grow well in these deep containers.

Plastic-coated fabric growing bags make great raised beds and suit small courtyards and patios where space is at a premium or fruit and vegetables are only grown in summer. They are tough, easy to move and store, and are available in a range of sizes, from 60cm (2ft) planters to substantial raised beds. Many bags have drainage holes, but it is essential to check for them before filling with compost. You can also buy woven willow surrounds that lend these practical bags a decorative cottage-garden style, adding to the beauty of an informal patio when filled with crops and flowers. Try planting leafy crops between towering sweetcorn and climbing squashes or beans, or pack smaller beds with herbs and colourful salad leaves. The bags are also deep enough to allow several tomato or pepper plants to produce good crops. After harvesting, empty out the compost and wash the bags in detergent and hot water, and reuse the following year.

Heat-loving crops will thrive in a raised bed set against a south-facing wall or fence. Plants like chillies, peppers, and aubergines, which may otherwise need the warmth of a greenhouse or windowsill indoors, will enjoy the conditions in a sunny bed. A brick wall provides the best backdrop, as it reflects extra heat during the day and releases stored heat at night, allowing exotic plants to thrive outside in cooler climates. They are also ideal for planting early spring crops and germinating many seeds because the compost in raised beds is relatively warm compared to the soil in the ground. The only drawback is that they will dry out quickly and need watering regularly.

Crop and flower combinations

Beautiful plants in their own right, fruit and vegetables can be combined with ornamentals to create striking container displays. Choose a few edible flowers, too, for delicious blooming pots.

Captions clockwise from left

Add welcome colour to productive containers and raised beds with an edge of flowering herbs, such as the tufted purple French lavender (*Lavandula stoechas*) shown here. Their flowers also mirror the form of the sweetcorn plants behind, and liven up the leafy potatoes, which can look a little dull on their own. Annual bedding plants, such as verbenas and salvias, are other good options and combine well with vegetables because they both enjoy full sun and are planted afresh each year. Their vivid colours also complement both leafy and fruiting crops, and scented French marigolds (*Tagetes*) may even help to deter pests. Also try sweet peas or other annual climbers in tandem with runner beans for taller displays.

Weave together fruit and blooms in rustic containers for a naturalistic look. Here, alpine strawberries make an informal edging for raised beds made from recycled crates. Their white flowers and tiny ripening fruits peep out beneath the tall potatoes, and unlike other forms of strawberry, they can tolerate the shade these plants cast. If growing larger fruit bushes and trees, which remain in their pots year after year, try partnering them with decorative perennials. For example, you can fill the gap between blossom time and ripe fruit by underplanting with a mist of blue catmint (*Nepeta*) or a carpet of pink *Geranium cinereum*. Add winter interest to fruit pots, too, by smothering the soil beneath a blackberry or fig tree with the colourful foliage of evergreen heucheras.

Decorate a table with an edible meadow, using herbs, salad leaves, and tasty flowers. Here, the planter is sunk into the table, but the display would look equally appealing in a window box set on top. Nasturtiums, pot marigolds (*Calendula*), and violas all have vibrant blooms that taste as good as they look, while herbs, including thyme, marjoram, and chives, have fragrant flowers as well as aromatic leaves. Ensure your planter has drainage holes, holds sufficient compost for good growth, and that the table can support the weight of the moist compost and plants.

Growing spaces under cover

Seeds can be sown earlier and crops harvested later if you can find a space for them under cover, and even the smallest cold frame or a tiny greenhouse can vastly increase your productivity.

Captions clockwise from top left

Pack crops into a tiny greenhouse to make the most of every inch of space. As well as pots of tomatoes, chillies, peppers, and aubergines, include a hanging basket or two planted with strawberries for an early crop. Also remember to leave space on staging for seed trays. In summer, open the door and vents in the morning to increase airflow, lower the temperature, and prevent a stagnant atmosphere, which will encourage diseases; close the greenhouse at night to retain heat. In addition, use blinds or apply special paint between spring and early autumn to shade plants from strong sun. Heating is not necessary to grow a range of summer crops and winter leaves, but to keep a greenhouse frost-free for citrus trees, insulate it well and use a temperature-controlled electric heater, rather than gas or paraffin burners, which need careful ventilation to remove the water and gases they emit.

Cold frames protect crops against the cold and wet and are ideal for small spaces. Place them against a sunny wall or in a sheltered, light area, and use them for germinating seeds, hardening off young plants, and growing crops such as squashes that do well with extra heat. Either prop the lid open or remove it to provide ventilation during the day, and close or replace it at night.

Make good use of space in a small greenhouse by setting your crops in staggered rows, like the tomatoes in crates shown here. Also keep tall plants, such as cucumbers, trained tidily onto their supports, with sufficient light and space around them to encourage the fruits to ripen. The space under staging can be used for pots of strawberries and herbs, if it's not too shady.

Set a mini greenhouse against a sunny wall to protect crops in a small garden, or on a balcony or terrace. These small greenhouses range from models with a light metal framework covered with plastic designed to protect tomatoes in a growing bag, to more expensive and versatile glazed metal- or wooden-framed structures, with shelves to accommodate seed trays as well as taller plants.

Getting started

Growing your own fruit, vegetables, and herbs in containers is easy, but working out where, when, and how to begin can be more challenging. The incredible range of crops on offer is enough to make anyone's head spin, and then you have to decide whether to grow them from seed or buy young plants. It's also important to select the right containers and compost to maximize your plants' potential and to create attractive displays. This chapter covers this essential information, and provides all the advice you will need to plan your productive container garden and get your crops off to a flying start. A quick-reference seasonal planner also offers guidance on when to sow and plant and, most importantly, when you can expect to reap the rewards.

Planning crops in pots

Where space is limited, plan your crops carefully to achieve a long cropping season and a lush, colourful container display at all times of the year. Selecting an appropriate site and a variety of crops that suit your needs, as well as having essential equipment to hand, will all help to ensure success.

Choosing a site

One advantage of growing in pots is that they can be moved into the sun or shade, from indoors to outside, or from an exposed site to a sheltered one. Most productive plants require full sun for at least part of the day, but consider the needs of individual crops because while sun-traps are ideal for ripening fruit, they cause leafy plants to wilt and increase the need for watering. Wind can also desiccate compost, damage plants and blow pots over, so avoid exposed sites if possible, or create some shelter around your crop display.

Sunny windowsills, porches and conservatories are great places to grow crops throughout the year. For example, citrus trees fruit best in a cool spot indoors during the winter (move them outside in summer). Keep areas indoors well ventilated during the summer months and protect young plants from intense light with shading or set them on a north- or east-facing windowsill.

Essential equipment

Container gardening does not require heavy digging or soil preparation, so there is no need for an array of large, expensive tools. Invest instead in a good-quality hand fork and trowel, which will be valuable for planting and weeding, along with secateurs for pruning and tidying plants. Also buy a watering can with a fine rose that will not displace the compost in your pots; a small can is useful for pots of seedlings.

A range of containers of all shapes and sizes will provide homes for your crops. Buy them from garden centres and DIY shops, but be imaginative too and create features from any suitable vessel that has some drainage holes at the bottom. Small pots, modules, and seed trays are also useful for raising your own seedlings.

Good-quality compost is obviously indispensable, but also remember labels, string, wire, cloches, fleece, netting, and supports, such as canes, pea sticks, and wigwams.

Sunny walls retain heat to help ripen fruit.

Buy module trays, labels, and a watering can for sowing seed.

Choosing crops for all seasons

For a display that is perennially bountiful, grow a wide range of fruit and vegetables and be poised with young plants to replace those that are no longer productive. This is not difficult to achieve with a little planning and by growing some plants indoors or under cloches outside.

Planning ahead is the key to success if you want a continuous crop over a long season. First, decide what you would like to eat, and then find out when those plants can be sown and harvested. Also select a range of crops that will keep the garden full, and you and your family fed, throughout the year. Try to mix plants that crop over a long season, like courgettes, perennial herbs, and Swiss chard, with quick-croppers such as radishes and salad leaves that mature in a matter of weeks, and can be sown every fortnight to fill gaps around plants that take longer to grow.

Protecting plants from the cold and wet allows you to extend the growing season in cooler climates. If you have space indoors or in a greenhouse, you can sow seeds earlier in spring and harvest crops later in autumn. Fleece and cloches provide sufficient protection for many plants on cold nights in spring and autumn, while an unheated greenhouse can be used for heat-loving crops, such as tomatoes, where summers are unreliable. Growing salads, herbs, and citrus trees on windowsills or bringing them into a cool conservatory will also prolong the harvest.

Spring

Most seed is sown in early spring, but any harvests at this time of year will be from overwintered crops. By late spring, however, sweet new-season treats will be ready to eat.

Harvest:
- Rosemary
- Radishes
- Peas
- Lettuce
- Rhubarb
- Beetroot
- Swiss chard

Summer

Soft fruits and young vegetables are ripe for picking in the summer. Also sow fast-growing crops every few weeks to crop at regular intervals and provide a continuous harvest.

Harvest:
- Basil
- Strawberries
- Potatoes
- Courgettes
- Tomatoes
- Blueberries
- Beans

Autumn and winter

Autumn brings a bounty of fruit and vegetables, many of which can be stored for leaner times. Winter crops can also be picked outdoors and on windowsills and in greenhouses.

Harvest:
- Chillies and peppers
- Apples and pears
- Potatoes
- Leeks
- Kale
- Witloof chicory
- Windowsill herbs

Choosing and buying seeds and plants

Growing vegetables used to mean raising them from seed, but thanks to their popularity, garden centres and mail-order companies now also offer a wide range of seedlings and young plants. Deciding what to buy is a question of how much time, money, and space you have, and which crops you have chosen to grow.

Seeds

Growing plants from seed is easy and immensely satisfying. Seeds are available from garden centres and mail-order companies, or collect them from plants that have been left to flower. Seeds offer the widest choice of vegetable cultivars, with options of size, habit, colour, and disease resistance. Potatoes are grown from tubers, known as seed potatoes, while miniature onion and shallot bulbs, called "sets", provide an alternative to seed.

● **Crop choices** All vegetables, but particularly root crops, which are best grown from seed. Alpine strawberries are the only fruit worth sowing.
● **Pros** Seeds are cheap, and a packet stored in cool, dry conditions can last several seasons. They also offer control over plant numbers and flexibility to sow little and often.
● **Cons** Seeds take time, require small pots or trays, and need space, especially tender crops that are sown indoors.

Plug plants

These small plants are grown in modules and can be bought in garden centres or through mail-order seed companies. They are a useful option where space is limited or conditions are not suitable for raising plants from seed and they offer good value for money. However, such small plants are delicate and will need potting up and watering as soon as you receive them, especially if they have arrived in the post.

● **Crop choices** No fruit but most vegetables are available as plugs, particularly those that are grown in quantity, such as salads and leafy crops like Swiss chard.
● **Pros** Quicker than sowing seed, plugs save time and space, and are economical, even for lots of plants.
● **Cons** The range of cultivars available is more limited than for seed. Plants need careful handling, potting on, and acclimatizing to new conditions to avoid losses.

Seeds provide great value for money and a good choice of crops.

Seedling plants, or "plugs", save time and are relatively inexpensive.

Young plants

Available from garden centres and mail-order companies, sturdy young plants grown individually in small pots offer gardeners the chance to try crops that may be too time consuming or difficult to grow from seed. If there is only space for one summer squash, or a single specimen of several tomato cultivars, then buying them as young plants makes sense. Look for strong, healthy plants that look stocky, bright green and well-watered. Carefully knock plants from their containers to check that the roots are not cramped and pot-bound, and plant out as soon as they are hardened off and conditions are suitable.

- **Crop choices** Good choices include strawberries and rhubarb, as well as a range of fruiting vegetables, such as tomatoes, peppers, chillies, cucumbers, and aubergines.
- **Pros** Larger plants make an instant impact and save the time and space needed to raise seedlings. They are valuable for heat-loving crops if you have nowhere indoors to sow and grow them on, and can be purchased after the frosts when they can be planted outside. They're also a good idea if you only need one or two plants.
- **Cons** This is an expensive way to grow vegetables, and there is a much more limited range of cultivars on offer. Plants must be acclimatized to outdoor conditions, too, so don't buy too early if your indoor space is limited.

Trees and shrubs

Most fruit grows on trees and shrubs, which can either be bought growing in containers or as field-grown "bare-root" plants, which are lifted and sold when dormant between early winter and early spring. This dormant season is also the best time to plant fruit trees and bushes, although pot-grown types can be planted throughout the year. Container-grown fruit is widely available, while bare-root plants are usually only available from specialist fruit nurseries via mail order. Always buy certified disease-free plants and check that trees are growing on a suitable rootstock for pots (*see pp.64–65*). If buying single specimens make sure they are self-fertile; if not, you will need a suitable pollination partner as well.

- **Crop choices** All fruit trees and bushes are available in these forms. Choose mature specimens that are ready to fruit if you want instant impact.
- **Pros** Bare-root plants are cheaper and offer a wider range of cultivars on dwarfing rootstocks. Container-grown trees and shrubs can be planted year-round, are widely available, and don't need planting immediately.
- **Cons** Bare-root plants are only delivered in winter and early spring and must be planted immediately. Container-grown trees tend to be more expensive, with fewer cultivars on offer. Old stock can also be pot-bound.

Young plants are ideal if only a few crops are required.

Buy fruit trees and bushes in containers for instant impact.

Container choices

Pots can add style to a plot or be purely functional, but they must hold enough compost to supply plants with sufficient water and nutrients, and have adequate drainage. Select containers that suit your style of garden and your choice of crops.

Terracotta and glazed pots flatter many fruit and vegetable plants. Terracotta is porous, and draws moisture from compost, drying it out quickly, while glazed pots stay moist for longer. Their weight is also useful for anchoring taller plants but they can be difficult to move, so plant them *in situ*. Look for pots with a frostproof guarantee and line them with bubble plastic for added protection.

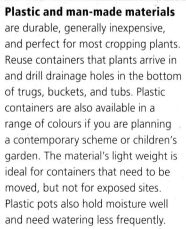

Plastic and man-made materials are durable, generally inexpensive, and perfect for most cropping plants. Reuse containers that plants arrive in and drill drainage holes in the bottom of trugs, buckets, and tubs. Plastic containers are also available in a range of colours if you are planning a contemporary scheme or children's garden. The material's light weight is ideal for containers that need to be moved, but not for exposed sites. Plastic pots also hold moisture well and need watering less frequently.

Metal pots make a stylish display and are practical too. Galvanised steel, with its resistance to corrosion, is a good choice for growing crops over many seasons, or you could improvise planters from old watering cans and large food tins, but be mindful of what was in them beforehand. Most metals are long-lasting and retain water well, but they also heat up quickly. This is an advantage for tender crops, but if you are growing salads that prefer cool conditions, line pots with bubble plastic before planting.

Wood and basketry brings a more rustic note to a productive display or adds formality, depending on the style of the container. Large half-barrels provide plenty of space for crops, old crates and wine boxes look good overflowing with plants, while elegant Versailles tubs suit pruned fruit trees. Woven materials are light and make beautiful hanging baskets, but they are not very durable. Wooden pots and baskets may need to be lined; if a liner is already in place, pierce it before planting to provide drainage.

Size matters when it comes to what's best for plants. In general, bigger is better. Larger containers hold more compost, and thus more moisture and nutrients, than smaller ones, making plants easier to look after. Herbs, such as thyme and marjoram, tolerate dry conditions and suit smaller pots, as do some fast-growing crops, like salad leaves. Trees and shrubs, as well as nutrient-hungry tomatoes, courgettes, and squashes, perform best in large pots, while deep containers are essential for root crops, such as carrots and potatoes.

Containers come in a range of styles that can all be exploited in a productive plot. Growing tables and mangers are raised planters that are a comfortable height for sowing and planting. Large hanging baskets and deep window boxes are ideal for trailing tomatoes, herbs, and flowers, while colourful woven bags are good for potatoes and courgettes. Grow bags can be used conventionally or cut in half to create two containers, and made more decorative with willow screens.

Preparing pots and compost choices

Plants grown in containers rely on you to provide them with a clean pot, drainage to prevent waterlogging, and a compost to suit their needs. Take time to prepare these ideal growing conditions and you will be rewarded with healthy, productive crops.

Choose good-quality compost that suits individual crops.

Preparing pots

Before planting, clean all pots, including new ones, with hot, soapy water to reduce the risk of transmitting diseases. To ensure that the compost does not become waterlogged, check that there are drainage holes in the base; if not, use a drill to make some. Terracotta pots benefit from a plastic lining to help prevent the porous clay drawing moisture from the compost. Metal pots can overheat in the sun, so line them with bubble plastic to keep the plant roots cool. Pierce the linings to provide good drainage.

Drill holes to provide drainage and line terracotta pots with plastic.

Supporting plants

Many tall and sprawling plants benefit from additional support to keep them healthy and cropping well. Fasten tall plants, such as cordon tomatoes and peppers, to sturdy canes or trellis with soft twine. Peas have tendrils that allow them to climb and grasp twiggy sticks and netting, while climbing beans will twist their stems around canes fashioned into a wigwam, but they may need tying in at first. Fruit trees and bushes trained as cordons or fans should be attached to taut wires or trellis as they grow.

Tie cordon tomatoes to a support; peas' tendrils will cling without any help.

Compost choices

There are many composts on the market and choosing the right one can seem complicated, but the decision is largely between soil-based and multipurpose types. Some multipurpose composts contain peat, but environmental concerns about peat extraction has led to substitutes, such as coconut fibre. Soil-based composts provide a steady supply of nutrients, and retain water and drain well. They provide good conditions for long-term growth and are particularly suitable for fruit bushes and trees. Multipurpose compost, with or without peat, is easy to use and lightweight; it's the best choice for hanging baskets but is not suitable for pots in exposed sites where they may blow over. It also dries out quite quickly and doesn't hold many nutrients, increasing the need to water and feed plants. However, multipurpose compost suits short-term crops, including many vegetables.

Seed compost is formulated for sowing and has a fine texture, which encourages high germination rates. It is also moisture retentive and low in nutrients, which is best for seeds.

Multipurpose compost is an excellent medium for both sowing and growing. It is ideal for annual vegetable crops that are fed and watered regularly.

Ericaceous compost is acidic, and should only be used for growing acid-loving plants. Of the fruits and vegetables featured, only blueberries require these specialized conditions.

Mulch options

Spreading a thick layer of material, known as a "mulch", on the compost surface looks attractive, helps to retain moisture, and prevents weed seeds from germinating. Mulches also help to prevent surface compost being washed away with repeated watering. Organic mulches, such as leaf mould, add nutrients and organic matter to the compost. Other options include bark chips, gravel, and slate, which provide a decorative touch. For maximum effect, apply a layer of mulch at least 2.5cm (1in) deep after watering the compost.

Mulches are both ornamental and functional, helping to conserve moisture.

Seasonal crop planner

Successful fruit and vegetable growing is all about good timing. Knowing the seasons to sow, plant, and harvest each crop, along with the quirks of your local climate and the rough dates of the last frosts, will help you to plan a container garden that is both productive and attractive throughout the year.

Early spring

As the weather warms and the days lengthen it's time to get sowing. Many crops can be sown outside now, but the warmth of a greenhouse or windowsill will give them a head start, and is essential for germinating tender crops.

Sow
- Outdoors: beetroot, carrots, chives, chop suey greens, coriander, corn salad, fennel, kale, kohl rabi, leeks, lettuce, onions, parsley, peas, radish, rocket, spinach, spring onions, Swiss chard, tarragon
- Under cover: alpine strawberries, aubergines, basil, beetroot, carrots, celeriac, cucumbers, dwarf French beans, lettuce, microgreens, peppers, rocket, sweetcorn, tomatoes

Plant
- Outdoors: chives, fruit trees and bushes, garlic, mint, onion and shallot sets, potatoes, rhubarb, tarragon
- Under cover: citrus trees

Harvest
Chives, kale, leeks, microgreens, parsley, rhubarb, rosemary, sage, Swiss chard, thyme, windowsill herbs

Sow carrots in early spring for a summer harvest.

Late spring

This is an exciting season, when everything is growing fast and baby vegetables are ready to harvest, but try not to get carried away. Crops like beetroot, carrots, lettuce, peas and radishes are best sown in small amounts every couple of weeks for a continuous harvest. Take care to harden off young plants (see p.36) before planting them outside, and protect vulnerable plants with fleece or cloches if cold nights are forecast.

Sow
- Outdoors: beetroot, French and runner beans, carrots, chicory, coriander, endive, Florence fennel, kale, kohl rabi, land cress, lettuce, mizuna, New Zealand spinach, oregano, oriental mustard, parsley, peas, radicchio, radishes, rocket, spring onions, sweetcorn, Swiss chard, thyme
- Under cover: aubergines, basil, French and runner beans, courgettes, cucumbers, microgreens, squashes, summer purslane, sweetcorn

Plant
- Outdoors: alpine strawberries, French and runner beans, celeriac, fennel, leeks, lettuce, mint, oregano, parsley, potatoes, rosemary, thyme
- Undercover: aubergines, citrus fruit, cucumbers, peppers, tomatoes

Harvest
Basil, beetroot, carrots, chives, chop suey greens, coriander, fennel, gooseberries, kohl rabi, microgreens, mint, oregano, parsley, peas, radishes, rhubarb, rocket, rosemary, sage, spinach, spring onions, strawberries, tarragon, thyme

Early summer

Summer arrives with a delicious glut of soft fruit, peas, and baby carrots. Net berries and currants to prevent birds getting to them first. Plant out tender crops when frosts have passed, and sow autumn and winter crops for harvests later in the year.

Sow

- Outdoors: French and runner beans, beetroot, carrots, chicory, chop suey greens, coriander, corn salad, courgettes, cucumbers, endive, kale, kohl rabi, land cress, lettuce, mizuna, oregano, oriental mustard, pak choi, peas, radicchio, radish, rocket, spinach, spring onions, squashes, sweetcorn, tarragon, Witloof chicory

- Under cover: basil, microgreens

Plant

- Outdoors: celeriac, courgettes, cucumbers, Florence fennel, kale, leeks, peppers, rosemary, squashes, sweetcorn, tomatoes

Harvest

Basil, beetroot, carrots, cherries, chives, chop suey greens, corn salad, courgettes, cucumbers, currants, fennel, gooseberries, herbs, kohl rabi, land cress, lettuce, microgreens, New Zealand spinach, oregano, oriental mustard, peas, early potatoes, radicchio, radishes, rocket, rosemary, spring onions, strawberries, Swiss chard

Late summer

This time of year yields a bumper harvest of tree and soft fruits and a huge range of vegetables. Check frequently to catch crops, such as beans, when they are small and tender. Leafy crops sown now, including Swiss chard and lettuce, can be harvested into winter if protected with cloches.

Sow

- Outdoors: beetroot, carrots, chop suey greens, coriander, corn salad, kale, kohl rabi, land cress, winter lettuce, mizuna, pak choi, oriental mustard, radicchio, radish, rocket, spinach, spring onions, Swiss chard, tarragon

- Under cover: microgreens

Plant

Kale, leeks, strawberries

Harvest

Apples, apricots, aubergines, basil, beetroot, blackberries, blueberries, carrots, cherries, chicory, chillies, chives, chop suey greens, coriander, corn salad, courgettes, cucumbers, currants, endive, fennel, figs, Florence fennel, French and runner beans, garlic, land cress, lettuce, microgreens, mint, mizuna, nectarines, New Zealand spinach, onions, oregano, pak choi, parsley, peaches, pears, peas, peppers, potatoes, radicchio, rocket, rosemary, sage, shallots, sweetcorn, tarragon, thyme, tomatoes, squashes, strawberries

Autumn

Harvest the fruits of your labours now to enjoy them fresh or to store for later. Later in the season, sow peas outside for an extra early spring crop, and bring herbs indoors.

Sow

- Outdoors: kohl rabi, land cress, winter lettuce, hardy peas, radishes, rocket

- Under cover: cut-and-come-again salad leaves, microgreens, rocket, alpine strawberries

Plant

Garlic, windowsill herbs, winter lettuce, strawberries

Harvest

Apples, apricots, aubergines, beetroot, black- and blueberries, carrots, celeriac, chicory, chives, chop suey greens, corn salad, courgettes, cucumbers, endive, fennel, figs, French and runner beans, herbs, kale, land cress, leeks, microgreens, mizuna, nectarines, onions, oriental mustard, pak choi, peaches, pears, peppers, potatoes, radicchio, radishes, rocket, strawberries, sweetcorn, Swiss chard, tomatoes, winter squashes

Winter

This is the quietest season, perfect for tidying, taking stock and planning for the year ahead. When the weather is not too cold most fruit trees and bushes can be planted and pruned. Garlic can also be planted, Witloof chicory forced for crisp salad leaves, and other hardy winter crops harvested, along with citrus fruit from the conservatory.

Sow

- Outdoors: hardy peas
- Under cover: microgreens

Plant

Fruit trees and bushes, garlic, rhubarb

Harvest

Celeriac, citrus fruits, corn salad, kale, land cress, leeks, winter lettuce, microgreens, mizuna, oriental mustard, parsley, rocket, Swiss chard, thyme, windowsill herbs, Witloof chicory

How to sow and plant

The basic techniques of sowing and planting are easy to master, and once you know how to get plants off to a good start, your only problem will be finding space for the containers to grow them. Begin by sowing quick and easy crops, like radishes, salad leaves, and herbs, and move on to those that are more demanding as your confidence grows. Before long you will have trendy microgreens on your windowsill, hanging baskets dripping with cherry tomatoes, and an elegant lemon tree to grace your patio in summer. This chapter guides you step by step through the methods for sowing seeds and planting out young plants. It also introduces a wide range of fruit and vegetables suitable for growing in pots, and includes all the details you will need to ensure they thrive.

Sowing seeds in trays

Growing crops from seed is simple and economical, and sowing in trays is a good idea as they are easy to clean and fit perfectly into propagators or on bright windowsills.

1 Clean used seed trays with hot water and detergent or soak in a sterilizing solution and rinse before you begin sowing. Fill a tray with multipurpose or seed compost, and use a second tray to gently firm it to remove air pockets.

2 Scatter seeds evenly over the compost, either straight from the packet or sprinkle them from the palm of your hand. Sow thinly to prevent waste and overcrowding, which results in spindly seedlings that are more prone to diseases.

3 Lightly cover the seeds with sieved compost and label the tray with the plant name and date. Water gently with tap water using a fine rose to avoid disturbing the seeds; avoid stored rainwater which can cause damping off disease.

Sowing seeds in trays *continued*

4 Place the tray in a propagator or cover it with clear plastic to create the warmth and humidity needed for germination. Keep in a light place, such as on a windowsill, but not in strong sun. Remove the cover as soon as seedlings emerge.

5 When the seedlings have a few leaves transplant them into module trays or small pots. To do this, water the seedlings, then hold a seed leaf and loosen the roots with a dibber or pencil to gently tease each one from the compost.

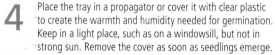

6 Have ready module trays or small pots filled with multipurpose compost, then water and allow to them to drain. Dibble a hole in each module, insert a seedling, and gently firm using the dibber. Water in and label.

7 After a few weeks, harden off the seedlings by gradually exposing them to the outdoor environment. Set them outside during the day and bring them in at night, or place them in a cold frame and gradually increase the ventilation.

Sowing seeds in small pots

1 Sowing in small pots works well for larger seeds and where fewer plants are required. Fill the pots with multipurpose or seed compost, firm gently and push the seed in to the correct planting depth. Label and water.

2 Cover pots with clear plastic, or put in a propagator until the seeds germinate. Thin seedlings to leave a single plant in each pot. Keep pots moist and turn those on windowsills daily to stop plants growing towards the light.

Tip for success: watering from below

3 Harden plants off gradually in a cold frame (*see opposite*) or place them outside during the day and bring them in at night. Plant them out into large pots before the roots become restricted, and water in well.

Watering trays and pots by placing them in a tray of water is a great way to prevent seeds and seedlings being disturbed and to ensure compost is thoroughly moistened. Leave containers in water until the compost surface feels damp, then remove and allow to drain.

Planting out young crops

When planting young crops like this chard, ensure your containers have holes at the bottom for good drainage, and that plants are well-spaced and firmed in.

1 Check that your container has adequate drainage holes in the bottom, and drill some if not. Cover the holes with a layer of broken clay pot pieces, and then fill the pot with multipurpose compost up to 5cm (2in) from the top.

2 Set out the plants in the pot while they are still in their own containers to check how many you need and that the spacing between them will be adequate. Water the plants well before carefully knocking them out of their pots.

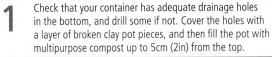

3 Make holes in the compost, allowing the correct distance between each plant (10cm (4in) for chard). Place a plant in each hole, check that the compost is at the same level around the plant as it was in its previous pot, and firm in.

4 Water the plants in thoroughly, using a rose on a watering can or a gentle spray setting on a hose, to settle the compost around the plants' roots. Continue to water the container regularly, particularly during hot weather.

Root crops

Easy to grow and wonderfully sweet when scrubbed and eaten fresh from the pot, most root crops thrive when sown outdoors, the seedlings thinned, and crops watered regularly. Choose deep pots to allow space for roots to develop.

Carrots

The long roots of carrots grow strong and straight in stone-free compost and their feathery leaves also look decorative in containers. Choose pots or growing bags that are at least 25cm (10in) wide and deep, and ensure drainage is good. Sow seeds every few weeks from early spring until late summer, either with quick-cropping early cultivars (round-rooted and short types do well in pots), or larger, slower maincrops which keep well. Depending on the shape of the pot, sow seed 1cm (½in) deep, in drills 15cm (6in) apart, or scatter thinly across the compost.

Aftercare and harvesting Once the first divided leaves appear, thin out seedlings to allow the remaining plants space to grow. Water consistently, but don't over-water as this causes leaves to grow at the expense of roots. Avoid carrot fly attacks by raising containers off the ground or creating a barrier. Harvest carrots from 12 weeks after sowing by pulling them gently from the compost.

1 Large, deep containers, such as these bags, are ideal for growing carrots. Ensure that the compost surface is level and make a shallow drill about 1cm (½in) deep, sow seeds thinly along it, cover with compost and water well.

2 When the seedlings have their first divided leaves, thin them to about 5cm (2in) apart, either by pulling them up between your fingers or snipping off the plants with scissors at soil level. Remove and compost all thinnings.

3 Carrot flies fly close to the ground and can be prevented from reaching your crops by creating a barrier with fleece that, together with the pot, is 60cm (24in) high, or by lifting the container the same height off the ground.

Beetroot

Make a feature of the clusters of red-veined leaves or combine them with other crops or flowers, and set pots in a sunny spot for good results. Although beetroots have spherical roots they still need a container at least 25cm (10in) deep to grow to a good size. Choose bolt-resistant cultivars in early spring and all other forms from mid-spring until late summer when plants are less likely to run to seed. Sow seed 2cm (¾in) deep and space evenly 5cm (2in) apart, planting some every few weeks for a constant supply of sweet roots throughout summer and autumn.

Aftercare and harvesting Beetroot seeds are actually a cluster of seeds that germinate to produce several plants, so thinning is always required, unless you select single 'monogerm' cultivars that require no thinning. Water plants consistently, and just enough to prevent the soil drying out. Small salad beets are ready to harvest from nine weeks, but large roots take up to three months to mature. Pull the roots gently from the soil and twist off, rather than cut, the stems to prevent bleeding.

Water beetroot regularly but avoid over-watering, which can lead to lush foliage and disappointing roots, and if drainage is poor, the leaves may wither and rot.

Pick summer radishes all together, as they will quickly run to seed if left in the soil. Harvest while they are small and sweet, and sow frequently to maintain your supply.

Radishes

An ideal crop for beginners, radishes are undemanding, fast-growing and particularly delicious when freshly picked. They germinate rapidly and are good for filling unexpected gaps, but they also tend to bolt in hot, dry conditions so place pots in some shade in summer. Sow summer cultivars outdoors from early spring through until autumn, covering early and late sowings with cloches if the weather turns cold. Sowing a small amount every two or three weeks gives a longer harvest and prevents gluts. Scatter seeds thinly or sow in rows 5cm (2in) apart at a depth of about 1cm (½in). Larger winter radishes are slower to mature. Sow in deep pots from mid- to late summer, 2cm (¾in) deep, with 15cm (6in) between rows.

Aftercare and harvesting Thin radishes promptly to make space for rapid growth: space summer radishes 2cm (1in) apart and winter types 10cm (4in) apart. Keep pots well watered since dry soil causes plants to bolt. Summer radishes can be ready to pick in as little as four weeks, while winter roots, such as 'Mantanghong', take several months, but they are hardy and can be left in the soil in cold weather. To harvest, pull roots gently from their pots.

Planting potatoes in a bin

Potatoes taste best when freshly harvested. Grow them in deep pots or bins like this, and plant "earlies", "second earlies", and "maincrops" for tubers over a long period.

Tip for success

The large, leafy potato plants and developing tubers need a reliable supply of water to produce a good harvest. Water pots regularly and never allow the compost to dry out.

1 Sprout ("chit") potatoes before planting. In early spring, place seed potatoes in egg boxes, with the end with the most eyes facing upwards, and set them on a cool windowsill. Plant when the shoots are 2cm (¾in) long.

2 From mid- to late spring, make drainage holes in the base of the bin and fill a third with compost. Evenly space five potatoes on the surface, with their shoots pointing up. Cover with 15cm (6in) of compost and water well.

3 Add compost around the plants in stages as they grow until the bin is full. Known as "earthing-up", this encourages more tubers to form, prevents them turning green and poisonous on exposure to light, and reduces frost damage.

4 With consistent watering, potatoes should be ready to crop when the plants flower. Empty the bin and harvest the tubers all at once or allow plants to continue growing and pick through the compost to take what you need.

Leafy crops

Lush, leafy vegetables flourish in pots and their decorative colours and shapes add drama to both garden and plate. Try red, speckled, green, ruffled, and oak-leaved lettuces, and cold-season crops like curly endive, blanched chicory, and crinkly kale.

Kale

One of the hardiest vegetables, kale leaves look beautiful and can be harvested throughout winter and early spring, when productive pots are in short supply. Seed is best sown from mid- to late spring in trays, and seedlings planted into final pots in early summer; young plants are also available at this time of year. Sow 2cm (¾in) deep and space young plants at least 15cm (6in) apart in large containers. Kale has a long growing season, requires space to mature, and needs a sunny situation to thrive.

Aftercare and harvesting Water crops regularly, especially while young plants are becoming established, and watch out for cabbage white butterfly caterpillars from mid- to late summer. Pick the lowest leaves on the stems and plants will remain productive for many months. An occasional liquid feed with a nitrogen-rich fertilizer is beneficial, particularly in early spring. Also remove and compost any lower leaves that turn yellow and fall.

Raise kale by sowing seed in trays and transplanting seedlings carefully into modules (known as "pricking out", *see p.36*). Or buy young plants and plant in their final pots.

Black Tuscan kale is a large decorative form with blistered, dark green leaves. Like all kales, it is vulnerable to bird and caterpillar attacks; protect with fine netting to prevent damage.

Endive and chicory

Late spring to midsummer sowings of endive and chicory produce crisp leaves that add a slightly bitter note to salads from midsummer until winter. Endive has relatively flat heads of curly leaves that can be blanched before harvest. Sow in modules and plant out 25cm (10in) apart in a good-sized pot. Set in light shade during summer.
   Witloof chicory is forced to produce pale hearts of leaves, known as "chicons". Sow in modules and then plant in deep pots, about 20cm (8in) apart, to allow the long roots to develop. Radicchio is a form of leafy chicory, and produces small hearts of red leaves. Sow seed thinly in a large pot and thin plants to 15cm (6in) apart.

Aftercare and harvesting Keep both crops moist in summer. Blanch endive by covering the central leaves when they are dry with a plate. Leave for 12 days and cut the whole head. Harvest radicchio between summer and late autumn, and blanch Witloof chicory in winter.

To force Witloof chicory, cut back leaves to 3cm (1½in) above the roots, exclude light with a pot, and set indoors. The blanched "chicons" will be ready in a few weeks.

Raising lettuces on a windowsill

For fresh salad leaves to hand whenever you need them, sow cut-and-come-again lettuces on a bright kitchen windowsill. Loose-leaf lettuce cultivars and many other types of salad leaves, such as mizuna and rocket, respond well to being sown quite thickly, the baby leaves cut, and the stumps allowed to regrow two or three times. Alternatively, allow the tender leaves to grow longer and snip off as required; more leaves will then grow.

1 Long, slim pots or fabric bags fit snugly onto a windowsill and look attractive with woven willow surrounds. Fill them with compost to about 1cm (½in) below the rim and make drills ½cm (¼in) deep and about 5cm (2in) apart.

2 Pour seed into the palm of your hand and sprinkle it into each drill using your thumb and forefinger. Cover the seeds lightly with compost and water thoroughly using a can with a fine rose to avoid disturbing the seeds.

Growing hearted lettuces

3 Keep the compost moist and when the seedlings are 5–10cm (2–4in) in height, cut them as required, about 2.5cm (1in) above soil level. The plants should then sprout new leaves which can be harvested about two weeks later.

Butterhead, cos, and crisphead lettuces all develop dense central hearts of leaves if left to mature, which look beautiful and provide generous crops for salads. Sow seed in trays and plant out the seedlings 20–30cm (8–12in) apart to allow them space to grow.

Designer leaves

Add a dash of style to your containers and dishes by growing a selection of gourmet leaf crops. Although expensive in the shops, they are cheap and easy to grow from seed, and their lively flavours are best when freshly picked.

Chard

An absolute must for every vegetable gardener, chard is a beautiful crop with a delicious earthy taste. It is also robust enough to withstand dry conditions and can even be harvested through mild winters. Seed can be sown into final pots, but raising seedlings in modules to plant out is often more successful. Sow seed 1cm (½in) deep, in late spring for a summer crop and in late summer for winter and spring leaves. Thin or plant out seedlings 10cm (4in) apart for baby leaves or up to 30cm (1ft) apart where impressive mature plants are desired. Choose a large pot, and place it in full sun or light shade for the best results.

Aftercare and harvesting Chard tolerates dry soil, but is happier when kept moist with regular watering. It crops over a long period if leaves are cut individually, allowing the youngest central leaves to continue to grow. Prevent cold weather damaging crops by covering them with cloches, although frosted plants will regrow in spring.

Chard's boldly coloured stems and leaf veins create a striking contrast with the light green leaves, making a decorative display in rustic or contemporary pots.

Exotic combinations of rocket and oriental leaves can be sown in a single pot of multipurpose compost to create a variety of leaf colour and texture for fresh salads.

Rocket and oriental leaves

Familiar from bags of supermarket salad leaves, the flavours of rocket, mizuna, and oriental mustard are fresher and feistier when plucked straight from the plant. Despite their high cost in the shops, these salads are easy and cheap to grow, and when given moist soil in sun or light shade baby leaves can be ready to crop in just three weeks. Scatter seed thinly over the compost, aiming for about 1cm (½in) between seeds, cover with ½cm (¼in) of compost and water well. Sow a batch of seeds outside every fortnight from mid-spring, and indoors from autumn until early spring for leaves all year round.

Aftercare and harvesting Keep compost moist, particularly during hot weather when plants run to seed quickly if they dry out. Pick leaves individually when they reach the desired size or cut the plants about 2.5cm (1in) above soil level and leave them to regrow. Both methods provide harvests over several weeks.

Cress and microgreens

The easiest crops to grow year-round, microgreens and cress can be grown in small pots or trays indoors, and are ready to harvest in a week or two. They make tasty additions to salads and sandwiches, as well as stylish contemporary garnishes for all kinds of dishes. What they lack in size they make up for with intensity of flavour, and you can buy a wide range of microgreen seeds, from herbs, such as basil and coriander, to rocket and broccoli.

1 To grow your own cress, add a layer of multipurpose compost to the bottom of a small pot, dish, or shallow seed tray. Then add a few layers of paper kitchen towel or cotton wool on top, which will retain plenty of moisture.

2 Add water to the pot, allowing time for it to soak into the layers of towel or cotton wool. Allow any excess water to drain from the pot before sowing the seeds. Prepare and sow a few pots to provide a decent-sized crop.

3 Pour seeds into your hand and sow them quite thickly and evenly over the surface of the pot. Press them down gently to ensure contact with the moist surface. Cover the pot or place in the dark to encourage rapid growth.

Growing microgreens

4 Once the seedlings are about 2.5cm (1in) in height, move them into the light and turn daily so that they grow evenly. Avoid bright sun, which may damage the leaves. Keep moist and after about a week cut the cress as required.

Microgreens take up to two weeks to crop, and are best grown in trays of compost. Try a range of salads and herbs by sowing thickly, covering the seed lightly with compost, watering well, and harvesting with scissors when the first young leaves have formed.

Beans and peas

Elegant flowers and a climbing habit make these crops ideal for large pots in small gardens. Bacteria in their roots provide them with their own source of nitrogen, but for plump pods they also need a steady supply of water.

Runner beans

With their lush foliage and bright scarlet flowers, runner beans are ornamental plants that can climb to more than 2.4m (8ft) in height. They are tender and need warmth to germinate, so for early crops sow indoors from mid-spring, or wait until late spring to sow into pots outside. Push the large seeds 5cm (2in) deep into the compost and allow 15cm (6in) between plants in their final positions. Choose a deep container, at least 45cm (18in) in diameter, and add sturdy supports about 1.8m (6ft) high for the plants to grow up. Beans flourish in a sunny, sheltered site. In more exposed gardens, grow dwarf cultivars, such as 'Hestia', that need no supports.

Aftercare and harvesting Runner beans need plenty of moisture to produce a good crop, so never allow pots to dry out. Tie young plants to their supports, and feed weekly with a tomato fertilizer when the flowers appear. Pick beans when young to encourage more crops to form.

1 To get runner beans off to an early start, from mid- to late spring plant single seeds about 5cm (2in) deep in small pots filled with multipurpose compost. Water well, and keep indoors or in a heated greenhouse to germinate.

2 Gradually acclimatize plants to outdoor conditions (*see p.36*) and plant out once the risk of frost has passed. Fill a large, deep container with compost and push tall canes into the pot, tying them together securely with twine.

3 Water the beans well, knock each from its pot, and place in holes made at the base of the canes. Fill around the roots, firm the compost, and water in well. Tie each bean to its cane to help it to start climbing.

French beans

Vigorous plants that crop reliably and prolifically, French beans are available as climbing and dwarf cultivars. Both types do well in containers, but neither tolerate frost and need warmth to germinate. Sow seed 5cm (2in) deep in small pots indoors in mid-spring, or in their final containers outside from late spring to early summer. Provide plants with a deep container at least 45cm (18in) in diameter and up to 20cm (8in) between plants for the highest yields. Remember to acclimatize young plants to outdoor conditions before planting them out (*see p.36*) and choose a sheltered site in full sun. Supports at least 1.8m (6ft) high are required for climbing cultivars, while bushy dwarf types need no support but sometimes also require propping up with sticks when laden with beans.

Aftercare and harvesting After planting, attach young plants to their supports (*see opposite*). Keep the compost consistently moist, and feed plants weekly with a tomato fertilizer when the flowers appear. Pinch out the growing tips of climbing beans when they reach the top of their supports to prevent a top-heavy tangle and to encourage a larger yield. Pick beans when young for the tenderest pods and to keep plants productive, or shell more mature pods for delicious green flageolet beans.

French beans and climbing flowers, like this bold black-eyed Susan (*Thunbergia alata*), enjoy similar conditions and add a burst of colour to productive pots.

Decorative pots of peas dripping with bright green pods liven up an edible patio display. When a little plumper, these immature pods will be ready to harvest.

Peas and pods

Delicious when eaten fresh, peas are easy to grow and highly productive. Grow shelling types for green peas, or try mangetout and sugarsnap cultivars that have edible pods. Early peas mature faster and are dwarf, requiring less staking, while tall maincrop cultivars take longer to crop but produce higher yields. Sow early types outdoors in early spring, or late winter in mild areas, then sow all other types in small batches fortnightly from mid-spring until early summer. Plant seeds 2.5cm (1in) deep, at least 5cm (2in) apart, in a deep pot with a minimum diameter of 30cm (12in), and place in a sunny, open site.

Aftercare and harvesting Protect seeds and seedlings from attacks by birds with netting, and set traps for mice. Plants also require light support with twiggy pea sticks or netting. Water pots consistently and feed weekly with a tomato fertilizer when the flowers appear. Pick pods while young for the best flavour and to encourage further crops.

Mediterranean-style vegetables

The jewel-like fruits of these decorative plants make beautiful displays in pots in a greenhouse, on a windowsill, or in a sunny, sheltered spot outside. Seek out compact cultivars and unusual types to add interest to your containers.

Peppers and chillies

A diverse group of plants, ranging from dwarf cultivars to those that reach 1m (3ft) in height, peppers and chillies are available in a huge variety of fruit sizes, shapes, and flavours. For the best results, grow them indoors or in a greenhouse, although fruit will ripen outside in mild areas or during a hot summer. Sow seed indoors in early spring and harden off young plants in time to plant out when the risk of frost has passed (*see p.36*). Allow a 20cm (8in) pot for each plant, smaller for dwarf cultivars, and place plants in a sheltered site in full sun.

Aftercare and harvesting Peppers and chillies should not be over-watered or fed excessively. Mist plants with water when they are in flower to help the fruit set and feed with a tomato fertilizer once a fortnight when the fruit has formed. Support plants that are fruiting heavily by tying stems to canes, and start picking when fruits are green and immature to encourage further crops.

Thin-skinned peppers that mature early are best for growing outside in cool climates. Either leave fruits to ripen on the plants or pick earlier and ripen indoors.

Chillies need heat to develop their full flavour, and will produce a large crop of ripe fruits when grown indoors on a sunny sill or in a greenhouse.

Harvest aubergines as soon as the fruits are plump and the skins are shiny and smooth. Cut the stems with secateurs or a knife, rather than pulling off the fruits.

Aubergines

Aubergines are pretty, bushy plants with slightly silvery leaves and fruits in various shades of purple, white, green, and orange. Good light levels and high heat are essential throughout their development, so only grow outdoors in mild areas in a sunny, sheltered spot. Sow seed in early spring indoors, either on a warm windowsill or in a heated propagator, and transfer young plants into larger pots as they grow. Finally plant into 20cm (8in) pots, and only place outside when the nights are frost free.

Aftercare and harvesting High humidity encourages fruits to set, so mist the purple flowers regularly or place pots on a tray filled with water and gravel. To encourage a bushier habit pinch out the main growing tip when plants reach about 20cm (8in). Once fruit starts to show, feed with a tomato fertilizer every two weeks, keep pots well watered and stake tall plants. Some cultivars are spiny so take care when harvesting them.

Growing tomatoes

Home-grown tomatoes taste divine and make beautiful displays in pots and hanging baskets when dripping with fruit. Cordons are tall and vigorous and need staking, while bush varieties are compact and require no training.

Cherry tomatoes will ripen outdoors, but beefsteaks need consistent heat and will be more productive when grown under cover. Sow seed indoors in early spring and pot on as plants grow, or buy young plants in late spring.

1 Once nights are frost free and plants are hardened off (*see p.36*), fill a pot, at least 25cm (10in) wide, with compost to 5cm (2in) below the rim. Plant the tomato deeply, as the section of buried stem will send out extra roots.

2 Tall cordon cultivars need training up a support. Push a couple of long bamboo canes or other sturdy stakes into the compost to keep the plant stable. Bush and trailing types do not need the help of supports.

3 As the plant grows, tie the main stems loosely to the canes using garden twine. Pinch out fast-growing sideshoots growing between the leaves and main stem on cordon cultivars. Leave sideshoots to develop on bush types.

4 Water regularly. When the first fruits appear feed weekly with a tomato fertilizer, and add extra compost if the roots become exposed. Pinch out the growing tip as the plant reaches the top of its cane. Ripe fruits twist off easily.

Decorative fruiting vegetables

Large leaves, golden flowers, and heavy yields make squashes, courgettes, and cucumbers ideal plants for productive pots. Combine them with the tall, elegant forms of sweetcorn for sweet and juicy fruits from summer to autumn.

Squashes

Fun to grow, both summer and winter squashes come in a wide variety of colours and sizes. They are hungry, fast-growing, trailing plants, but there are also smaller bush types and less vigorous climbers that are more suited to pots. Sow seed 2.5cm (1in) deep indoors in small pots in mid-spring or outdoors under cloches in late spring. Harden off plants (*see p.36*) before planting in large pots of multipurpose compost mixed with rotted manure. After the frosts have passed, place pots in a sunny site, and cover young plants with cloches during cold spells.

Aftercare and harvesting Water well and feed weekly with tomato fertilizer about a month after planting. Limit winter squashes to three fruits per plant so they reach a good size; you can leave all the fruits on summer forms. Harvest summer squashes from midsummer and eat fresh. To store winter types, from late summer leave skins to harden in the sun, and cut the stems before the first frosts.

Summer squashes include custard whites (*above*), patty pans, and scallop forms. Pumpkins, butternuts, and the small green and white 'Sweet Dumpling' are winter types.

Colourful woven bags make good homes for courgette plants and all forms of squash. These strong plastic bags can be washed and reused year after year.

Courgettes

These summer vegetables are incredibly productive, and most have a bushy, rather than trailing, habit, making them perfect for small spaces. Courgettes need warmth to grow well and will not tolerate frost, so sow indoors, 2.5cm (1in) deep in small pots in mid-spring, or wait until warmer late spring weather to sow outside. Gradually acclimatize young plants to outdoor conditions (*see p.36*) before planting out into large pots or growing bags when there is no risk of frost. Place in a sunny, sheltered spot.

Aftercare and harvesting Courgettes are fast-growing plants and need a plentiful supply of water to keep them healthy in containers. They also require feeding every week with a tomato fertilizer. Once flowering is underway the fruits develop rapidly, so check daily to catch courgettes while they are small and sweet, because when missed they seem to turn into marrows almost overnight. Cut fruits with a knife or twist firmly near the stem.

Sweetcorn

Sweetcorn grown in pots will not produce enormous yields, but the tall plants are beautiful and fresh cobs temptingly sweet and tender. Intolerant of frost, the fruits need a long, warm season to ripen, so start early by sowing seed in module trays indoors in mid-spring or outdoors under cloches in late spring. Never sow into cold, wet soil, as this will produce poor results. Harden off young plants (*see p.36*) and plant out at least 25cm (10in) apart in large containers filled with multipurpose compost. Place pots on "feet" to raise them off the ground, which ensures the good drainage these plants require, and stand in a sheltered site in full sun. Group plants together in blocks for good pollination, unless growing mini corn, which does not need to be pollinated.

Aftercare and harvesting Water consistently to produce juicy kernels, but only expect one or two cobs per plant. Mini corn is ready when the tassels at the cob tips start to emerge. Mature cobs are ripe when the tassels turn brown and the kernels are pale yellow. Pick when ripe and use immediately or freeze.

Sow sweetcorn seed thinly in trays, pushing them just beneath the surface, and wait until the roots have reached the bottom of the tray before planting out.

Plant corn and flowers for a pretty container display, or make use of the space below the slender leaves for quick crops, such as radishes.

Small-fruited cucumber cultivars are popular because they produce a succession of fast-maturing, tasty fruits in summer. Many also offer good disease resistance.

Cucumbers

Cucumbers have a reputation for being difficult to grow, but given warm, sheltered conditions and fertile, well-drained compost, outdoor ridge types are otherwise undemanding. The smooth-skinned longer types need more heat and must be grown under cover, ideally in a conservatory or greenhouse, as they need space to mature. If pollinated their fruit is bitter, so choose "all-female" cultivars bred to prevent this problem. Sow the seed of both types of cucumber indoors in mid-spring, 2.5cm (1in) deep in small pots. Harden off ridge cucumbers (*see p.36*) and plant outside when the risk of frost has passed. One plant will fill a large pot.

Aftercare and harvesting Protect from slugs after planting outside and cover young plants with a cloche in cold weather. Once established, cucumbers quickly become sprawling plants and are best trained up trellis, canes, or netting. Water well and feed weekly with tomato fertilizer once the first fruits can be seen forming behind the faded blooms. Pick fruits as they mature from midsummer to encourage the production of more.

Onions, garlic, and leeks

Indispensable in the kitchen, onions and their pungent-flavoured cousins are a must for every productive plot. Pots will not supply huge harvests, but the juicy flesh and subtle flavour of freshly picked crops outclasses shop-bought varieties.

Onions

These bulbs have shallow roots, making them good candidates for containers. Their strong scent also reputedly confuses pests, such as carrot fly, so mingle them among your other crops. Choose a large pot for a worthwhile crop, place it on "feet" to ensure good drainage, and site in a sunny position outside. Fill pots with multipurpose compost and sow seed 2cm (¾in) deep in spring. Thin seedlings to about 10cm (4in) apart. Onions are also easy to grow from small bulbs called "sets". Simply push them into compost in spring, about 10cm (4in) apart, so that just the tip is showing.

Aftercare and harvesting Keep the compost moist, but don't over-water or feed excessively, as this encourages soft growth which can be prone to rots. Harvest fresh, juicy bulbs throughout summer as required, or allow the leaves to yellow and die down naturally, then lift the bulbs and dry them in the sun before storing.

Grow onions in pots of fresh compost each year to avoid pest and disease problems that can build up in the soil. Plastic tubs are ideal, too, as they are easy to clean.

Garlic

Grow garlic for an early summer crop of succulent, mild-flavoured "green" or "wet" garlic, or wait until late summer to harvest and dry mature bulbs. Place a large, deep pot in full sun on "feet" to ensure it is well drained, and fill with multipurpose compost. Garlic is grown from cloves rather than seeds and needs exposure to a cold spell. Push firm, healthy cloves 2.5cm (1in) deep into the compost, with the pointed end facing upwards, either in autumn or late winter. Space the cloves 15cm (6in) apart.

Aftercare and harvesting Keep well watered, as garlic is a surprisingly thirsty crop, but do not allow the compost to become waterlogged or the bulbs will rot. For fresh green garlic, lift in early summer or, for mature bulbs, wait until the leaves begin to yellow later in the summer. Then dry the garlic for about a week indoors or outside in the sun, before cutting off the stems and storing. Alternatively, plait the stems for a traditional garlic string.

Plant garlic cloves by late winter so that they have produced strong green foliage by early spring. Water well and they will develop plump bulbs to use fresh or to store.

Growing leeks

Hardy and delicious, leeks are a valuable crop for autumn and winter, but they need a long growing season and tie up space for many months. Early, mid-, and late season cultivars are available. Early leeks crop in autumn and are less hardy, while mid- and late types are stockier and will sit in cold soil until you're ready to harvest them. Seed for all types can be sown directly into pots, but it's best sown in trays in spring for transplanting about ten weeks later.

1 In spring, sow seed thinly, about 1cm (½in) deep, in a tray on a windowsill indoors. Water the tray well and do not allow it to dry out. When the seedlings are approaching 20cm (8in) tall harden them off (*see p.36*).

2 Once the leeks are hardened off, fill a large container with multipurpose compost. Gently ease each leek from the seed tray using a dibber or pencil, and trim any long straggly roots with scissors to make transplanting easier.

3 Make holes 15cm (6in) deep and drop a leek into each. Space plants 10–20cm (4–8in) apart; a wider spacing should result in larger leeks. Pour water into each hole and the compost will slowly fill around the stem to blanch it.

4 Make sure the compost is kept moist and apply a liquid feed every few weeks. Add extra compost around the plants as they grow to produce long, white, blanched stems. Harvest when the leeks are large enough.

Stems and roots

Slightly weird and wonderful, these quirky crops look appealing in containers and have their own distinctive flavours.

Often expensive to buy or difficult to find in shops, planting these delicacies at home is sure to repay your efforts.

Rhubarb

Eaten as a fruit, but officially a vegetable, rhubarb is a big deep-rooted perennial that will grow in a large pot for several years. Its blush stems and green sculptural leaves make an impressive architectural feature too. Plant young rhubarb plants or "crowns" in early winter or early spring. Pots require good drainage to prevent plants rotting, but the large leaves also need a steady supply of water, so mix well-rotted manure with the compost when planting, and keep pots moist. In early spring, apply an all-purpose granular fertilizer and renew the top layer of compost.

Aftercare and harvesting Pick stems from spring until early summer by twisting and pulling at the base rather than cutting them off, but do not harvest them in the first year to allow plants to bulk up. Tender, pale pink, forced stems are an early spring delicacy and are produced by excluding light from the plant. Forcing exhausts plants, however, so give them a rest every other year.

1 Choose a large pot, at least 30cm (12in) wide, with drainage holes, and cover the base with broken clay pot pieces. Fill with compost mixed with rotted manure; add water-retaining crystals to help keep the compost moist.

2 Make a hole in the compost and plant the rhubarb; ensure the crown, where new shoots emerge, is not buried. Keep well watered. Each spring, refresh the top layer of compost and add some granular fertilizer at the recommended rate.

3 To force rhubarb for pale pink, sweet stems, exclude light completely by placing a bucket, or terracotta forcing pot, over the plant at any time from late winter until early spring. Blanched stems will be ready about a month later.

Kohl rabi

Beautiful to look at, good to eat and easy to grow, kohl rabi is the perfect crop for a small container garden. Plants are grown for their swollen stems, which have crunchy, sweet, white flesh and purple, green, or white skins. Sow small quantities every two or three weeks from early spring until late summer, either directly into large pots or into module trays or small plastic pots outdoors to fill spaces later in the season. Sow seed about 1cm (½in) deep, and thin or plant out 10–20cm (4–8in) apart, depending on the size of kohl rabi you require. Water in well and place the final container in full sun.

Aftercare and harvesting Keep the compost moist by watering regularly to promote fast growth. Protect early sowings with cloches if the nights are cold, as this may cause plants to bolt. Kohl rabi is ready to harvest in as little as ten weeks; pick when the swollen stems are about the size of tennis balls, before the flesh becomes woody. They also tolerate light frosts, the purple types being the hardiest, and late crops can often be picked through autumn and into winter. To harvest, simply pull the stems from the compost. Both the swollen stems, which have a mild turnip taste, and the leaves can be eaten raw in salads, or stir-fried or steamed.

Decorative and delicious, kohl rabi are trouble-free – just protect them from slug damage – and their swollen stems make fascinating specimens for pots.

Buy healthy young celeriac plants in late spring, as they can be difficult and time-consuming to grow from seed and you will only need a few to fill a container.

Celeriac

The odd appearance of this knobbly, swollen root belies its rather sophisticated mild celery flavour. The fact that it needs a long growing season and a continuous supply of water to reach a good size means that it is not the easiest plant to grow in pots, but adventurous gardeners and gourmets should find a space to try. Sow indoors in modules on the surface of the compost in early spring, or buy young plants later in the season. Pot on into larger containers and harden off to plant out in late spring or early summer (see p.36). Plant in a large pot, with about 25cm (10in) between plants.

Aftercare and harvesting Water regularly, and do not allow the compost to dry out in hot weather. Feed plants weekly with a fertilizer for root crops, and remove the oldest leaves when the celeriac starts to swell at the base of the stems. Lift the roots from autumn and through winter, and eat the celery-flavoured leaves too.

Culinary herbs

Essential recipe ingredients, herbs are great for beginners. Many will grow in the tiniest of spaces in hanging baskets, on windowsills, and among other crops.

Choosing herbs

If you have never grown herbs before, start with a selection of perennials, such as thyme and marjoram. Adapted to hot, dry conditions, these plants need free-draining soil and full sun for strongly scented leaves. Mint and chives are easy to grow, too, and will tolerate moist soil and some shade. Batches of annual herbs, like basil and coriander, can be sown from spring onwards for a continuous supply. Sow parsley in early spring, or buy young plants, for leafy crops throughout the year until the following spring, when the plants will run to seed.

Aftercare and harvesting Although herbs like good drainage, keep the compost moist, since many will run to seed rapidly if allowed to dry out. Use herbs at every opportunity because regular picking keeps plants bushy and encourages fresh new growth. Place pots on sunny windowsills indoors in autumn for fresh winter supplies.

Fill a hanging basket with a range of undemanding herbs, such as basil, marjoram, curry plant, and chives, to make a bold display of foliage colour, texture, and taste.

Growing shrubby herbs

Bay, rosemary, and sage all grow into attractive shrubs, and make decorative evergreen container specimens. Sage and rosemary are both fast-growing, so start with small plants and repot as they mature. Bay takes longer to grow, and it is worth investing in larger plants, especially if you want to train one into topiary. Plant shrubby herbs in soil-based compost, such as John Innes No 2, and place pots on "feet" to allow good drainage. Set in full sun.

Aftercare and harvesting Trim rosemary and sage after flowering to keep plants compact and encourage a flush of tender new leaves. Clip the tips of bay shoots to maintain a tidy, bushy form. Water plants regularly and protect bay and rosemary with fleece in cold winters.

Trained bay trees with plaited stems and bushy heads make beautiful edible sculptures. Repot into slightly larger containers every two years to keep them healthy.

Planting a herb pot

A single pot can provide a temporary home for an exciting range of herbs for the kitchen and the evergreens will look good throughout the year. Use a few bedding plants to add colour and complement the herbs' spring and summer flowers, and choose plants that all grow well in the same conditions. Do not include mint, which spreads vigorously and will overwhelm the other plants, and repot all the herbs into larger containers after a season or two.

1 Choose a large container with holes in the sides for trailing plants and drainage holes in the base. Add some broken clay pot pieces to the bottom, and fill with multipurpose or soil-based compost to just below the holes.

2 Creeping and trailing plants will slot perfectly into the holes. Knock them from their pots, roll the leafy stems in newspaper to protect them and push them through the holes. Remove the newspaper and repeat for each hole.

3 Add compost to cover the roots and firm well. Level the surface and try out different arrangements of herbs on top while they are still in their pots. Consider their final heights and spreads before settling on a design.

4 Water the herbs, remove them from their pots and plant in their final positions. Fill around the root balls with compost, ensuring stems and leaves are not buried, and firm in. Stand the pot in its final position and water well.

Summer berries

The true tastes of summer, strawberries and blackberries are a real treat to pick fresh from the garden. The plants grow happily in containers, provided they are watered well and you get to the juicy berries before the birds and mice do.

Blackberries

Closely related to the rampant, prickly brambles found in hedgerows, many modern blackberry cultivars are more compact, thornless, and produce larger, sweeter fruits. Choose these forms for containers, and they will repay you with delicate white flowers followed by heavy crops of late-summer berries. Blackberries are perennials and are best planted in early winter or early spring. Plant in a 45cm (18in) pot and soil-based compost, such as John Innes No 2, and set in full sun or partial shade.

Aftercare and harvesting Even on compact cultivars the arching stems require tying into canes or trellis, which can also be used to secure netting to protect fruit from birds. Do not allow pots to dry out and pick berries when they turn black and glossy. Prune out stems that bore fruit at the base, and tie in new stems to canes. In spring, refresh the top layer of compost, mixed with an all-purpose granular fertilizer; repot plants every two years.

Robust and vigorous, blackberries experience few pest problems and tolerate a wide range of conditions, making them the perfect choice for beginners.

Strawberries have long fruiting stems that create a decorative display of ripening fruits when planted at different levels in specially designed strawberry pots.

Strawberries

Rich red, syrupy, and sweet, strawberries really do taste better eaten straight from the plant when still warm from the sun. Conventional varieties fruit for about three weeks, so grow early, mid- and late season types, if you have space, for crops throughout summer. Alternatively, try perpetual or "ever-bearing" cultivars that fruit sporadically from late summer until the first frosts. Strawberries are sold as young plants and should be planted from late summer to early autumn for a good crop the following year. Plant several in a large container with good drainage, and place in full sun.

Aftercare and harvesting Keep compost moist and feed plants fortnightly with tomato fertilizer once berries have formed. Cover ripening fruit with netting to protect it from birds and pick as soon as the fruits have turned bright red. Plants are prone to disease and become less productive with age, so replace every three years.

Planting a basket of strawberries

Hanging baskets are a great way to make extra space for crops in small gardens or on patios, and look particularly beautiful when overflowing with ripe strawberries. The sweet fruits tempt many pests, particularly slugs and birds, both of which find it difficult to reach them when plants are suspended in the air. There is also no danger of fruits rotting due to contact with wet soil, and the ripe berries are easy to harvest, as long as the basket is not too high.

1 Place the basket in a pot to keep it stable while planting, and if it doesn't have an integral liner, line with durable plastic to retain compost and moisture. Cut drainage holes in the liner to prevent compost becoming waterlogged.

2 Water the plants in their pots. Add multipurpose compost to the base of the basket, mixing in water-retaining crystals if desired, and arrange plants so that the top of the root balls are 2.5cm (1in) below the basket rim.

3 Fill around the plants with more compost, firming as you go. Ensure the basket is not filled to the rim, leaving space for watering, and that the strawberries are not planted deeper than they were in their original pots.

4 Soak the basket well and allow the water to drain before suspending it from a sturdy and well-secured bracket or hook. Water daily in warm weather and apply a liquid tomato fertilizer every two weeks once fruits appear.

Currants and berries

Fruit bushes, including many berries and currants, are reliably productive and sparkle with colourful crops for most of the summer. Given large pots they will grow into substantial shrubs that need little pruning to maintain good harvests.

Blueberries

Worthy of a place in any garden, blueberries are attractive bushes with fresh green foliage, clusters of white, urn-shaped flowers and heavy crops of plump, blue-black berries from midsummer into autumn. Plant them in autumn or spring in acid soil, which is easy to provide by filling containers with ericaceous compost, and place pots in full sun or part shade. Some blueberries are self-fertile, allowing solitary plants to produce fruits, but yields tend to be better where several bushes are grouped together.

Aftercare and harvesting Keep the compost moist and apply a liquid ericaceous fertilizer once a month during the growing season. Also repot plants into slightly larger containers every two years. Blueberries have few pest and disease problems, but birds enjoy the fruits, so protect bushes with nets. Although regular pruning is not essential, cut back dead or damaged stems to the base of the plant in winter. Pick berries as they ripen.

1 Cover the base of a 38cm (15in) pot with broken clay pot pieces and a layer of ericaceous compost. Plant the blueberry at the same level as before by placing its pot in the container, filling around it with compost, and firming.

2 Remove the plastic pot and carefully place the plant into the remaining hole. Firm around the root ball to remove any gaps and dress the top of the pot with a little more ericaceous compost. Water the plant in thoroughly.

3 Place the pot in sun or light shade and cover with netting to prevent birds eating the developing berries. A cane wigwam with garden netting stretched over it is secure, but easy to remove and replace when picking fruit.

Gooseberries

Although the fruit can be difficult to find or expensive to buy in the shops, gooseberries are easy to grow in containers. Plant in 38cm (15in) pots during the dormant season, between late autumn and late winter, in a soil-based compost, such as John Innes No 2. Bushes stay healthy and fruit ripens best in a sunny spot with good air circulation, but they can tolerate some shade. Gooseberries are self-fertile and can be grown as single plants. They also respond well to being trained up walls or fences as cordons, which look great and save space.

Aftercare and harvesting Do not allow the compost to dry out and water plants regularly, but not heavily, in dry weather to prevent the fruits splitting. Apply a liquid tomato fertilizer fortnightly when the plant comes into leaf. Gooseberries can be picked from early summer, although their sweetness and flavour develops the longer they are left on the bush. Net plants to protect ripening fruits from birds; American gooseberry mildew and gooseberry sawfly are common problems in gardens.

Green-fruited gooseberries have a sharp taste and are best cooked with some sugar, while the red varieties are sweet enough to eat straight from the bush.

Currants

These tough shrubs grow vigorously and require large containers, at least 45cm (18in) wide and deep. They crop heavily in summer, and the fruit makes delicious preserves and freezes well for use later in the year. Plant currants from late autumn to late winter in soil-based compost, such as John Innes No 2, and place in a sheltered spot in full sun or partial shade. Plant blackcurrants deeply and straight after planting cut all the stems back to within 5cm (2in) of the soil to encourage new shoots to form. Prune the branches of red- and whitecurrants back by half after planting. Keep plants well watered, and feed fortnightly with a tomato fertilizer from spring to early summer.

Redcurrants Glorious when draped with strings of ruby-red berries, train the long stems on wires against walls or fences where space is limited.

Blackcurrants An essential fruit for puddings and jams, modern, compact cultivars are best for containers and boast superior flavour.

Whitecurrants These delicate, translucent berries are difficult to find in the shops and have a bold, sharp flavour similar to redcurrants.

Fruit trees for pots

Given the right care, many fruit trees flourish in containers and produce generous crops. Choose trees grafted onto dwarf rooting stocks, or buy one of the specially bred compact cultivars.

Choosing and planting trees

Ideal trees for pots are not too vigorous and self-fertile, which means you can grow one on its own and it will still crop well. Apples, pears, plums, cherries, figs, peaches, nectarines, and apricots will all thrive in pots when watered well. Choose trees grafted onto dwarfing rootstocks, such as M9 for apples or Pixy for plums and apricots. Very dwarfing rootstocks, such as M27 for apples, are not so successful when restricted to pots. Plant in containers about 50cm (20in) in diameter and use a soil-based compost, such as John Innes No 2. Place pots on "feet" to ensure good drainage, set trees on a warm, sheltered patio, and keep the compost moist at all times.

Aftercare and harvesting Apply an all-purpose granular fertilizer each spring and repot trees into slightly larger containers each year until they reach their final size. The heat radiated by a south-facing wall helps fruit like peaches and figs to ripen, but pots will need extra water.

Dwarf peach cultivars Ideal for growing in pots, bring these plants indoors from midwinter to protect the blooms from frost and reduce the risk of peach leaf curl (*see p.109*). Dust the flowers with a soft brush to aid pollination, and thin developing fruits to one per cluster.

Figs Trees do well in pots where their restricted root growth encourages more fruit. Set pots against a sunny wall and provide shelter in winter. In late autumn remove green fruits that have failed to ripen, but leave the tiny embryo fruits.

Cherries These vigorous trees are best trained as a fan against a wall or fence. Net pot-grown trees to protect fruits from birds, and after harvesting, prune back the fruiting stems to young sideshoots or new buds.

Apricots Reliable summer heat is needed for trees to fruit well. Grow against a sunny wall and protect the blossom from frost with fleece. Remove the fleece on warm days so insects can pollinate the flowers.

Planting an apple tree in a pot

Apples, like many fruit trees, make beautiful features, with their delicate spring blossom and colourful crops. Plant in large pots with drainage holes, place in a sunny site, and provide shelter from the wind to allow insects to pollinate the flowers and prevent containers blowing over. Choose a young two- or three-year-old tree that is grafted on a dwarf rootstock (*see opposite*) and has already been partly pruned into its final form, and keep trees well watered.

1 Add a layer of broken clay pots or gravel over the drainage holes, followed by soil-based compost mixed with a slow-release fertilizer applied at the recommended rate.

2 Water the tree, knock it from its pot, and check that the top of the root ball will sit 5cm (2in) below the new container's rim. Tease out roots to help them establish.

3 Position the tree carefully in the centre of the container. Fill around it with compost and firm, making sure that it is planted at the same level as in its original pot.

4 Water well, and apply a mulch of well-rotted manure or compost, leaving a space around the stem. Never allow the compost to dry out, but guard against waterlogging. Cut out dead and diseased wood as soon as you see it.

Citrus trees

Ideal for pots, citrus trees are prized for their glossy evergreen leaves, fragrant white flowers, and colourful fruits. Move them indoors in winter to provide the warmth needed for the fruits to ripen, but set them outside again in summer.

Potting up a calamondin tree

Highly ornamental dwarf citrus trees, calamondins bear small, round, mandarin-like fruits, which are produced throughout the year. They have sour flesh, and are perfect for adding to drinks or making marmalade. Plant trees in a soil-based compost, such as John Innes No 2, or a specialist citrus compost, and apply a mulch after watering to help retain soil moisture. Place pots in full sun and shelter them from cold winds and draughts.

Aftercare and harvesting Calamondins are quite hardy and able to tolerate light frosts, but need gentle heat year-round to yield fruits. Site in a cool and bright area indoors over winter and move outside onto a sunny patio when there is no longer a risk of frost. Keep the roots moist, but never waterlogged, by standing pots on "feet", and apply a summer citrus fertilizer fortnightly between spring and autumn, and a winter citrus fertilizer fortnightly the rest of the year. Repot trees annually until mature.

1 Select a container about 8cm (3in) wider than the root ball. Good drainage is key to successful citrus cultivation, so drill drainage holes in the base if the pot does not already have them. Water the calamondin well.

2 Cover the base with broken pot pieces to aid drainage and cover them with a layer of compost. Knock the tree from its pot and position so the compost will be level with the top of the root ball. Fill in with compost around the plant.

3 Firm the compost, and water thoroughly. Add a generous layer of mulch, at least 2.5cm (1in) thick, to help retain moisture. To increase humidity, which citrus trees need, stand the container on a tray filled with water and gravel.

Lemons fruit all year if given a cool area indoors in winter and warmth in summer. However, they do not thrive in warm, centrally heated conservatories in winter.

Lemons

Few plants are more handsome than a fruiting lemon tree in a classic terracotta pot. Where the temperature can be maintained above 11°C (52°F), they will remain in growth all year, giving a simultaneous display of starry, deliciously scented white flowers and ripening fruits. Like all citrus trees lemons are self-fertile, which means that a lone plant will produce fruits without a partner. Sharp drainage is essential, so ensure pots have holes in the base, add a layer of broken clay pot pieces beneath the compost (*see Step 2 opposite*), and set containers on "feet". Plant in soil-based compost, such as John Innes No 2 or a specialist citrus compost, and place in a sunny situation, whether under cover or in a sheltered area outdoors.

Aftercare and harvesting Lemons are killed by frost, and must be brought indoors before temperatures dive. They are best returned outdoors for summer because they do not enjoy excessive heat. Water once the top layer of compost is dry, but do not let them dry out completely, or they will drop their leaves. Feed with specialist citrus fertilizers as for calamondins (*see opposite*).

Oranges

All types of oranges thrive in large containers, but none tolerate frost. Sweet oranges, including blood and navel cultivars, need temperatures of around 18°C (65°F) to ripen and develop their full flavour. Sour or Seville oranges are not as tender, and their acidic fruits are ideal for making marmalade. Provide a pot with a few drainage holes in the bottom to prevent waterlogging, and plant up using a soil-based compost, such as John Innes No 2 or a specialist citrus compost. Position trees in full sun, shelter from wind, and protect from cold draughts when growing plants indoors.

Aftercare and harvesting Avoid exposing orange trees to extreme temperature fluctuations by keeping them in a cool, bright conservatory or heated greenhouse in winter and a sheltered position outside in summer after the risk of frost has passed. Increase humidity indoors by placing the pot on a tray filled with water and gravel. Water when the compost surface is dry and feed with specialist citrus fertilizers as for calamondins (*see opposite*). The fruits can take up to six months to reach their full size and ripen.

Harvest oranges from early winter through to spring. For a good crop, try to mimic the cool winters and warm summers of the Mediterranean regions where they thrive.

Recipe collections

Productive plants offer an amazing array of foliage and flowers that can be used in a range of ornamental edible displays. Whether you have a tiny window ledge, sunny patio, or large garden, transform your plot into a container kitchen garden with the recipes in this chapter. Designed to make the most of your space, they include crops that can be harvested from spring to autumn.

Key to plant symbols
Soil preference

◌	Well-drained soil
◍	Moist soil
◌ ◍	Well-drained or moist soil

Preference for sun or shade

☼	Full sun
☼	Partial or dappled shade
☼ ☼	Either full sun or partial shade

Hardiness ratings

✿ ✿ ✿	Fully hardy plants
✿ ✿	Plants that survive outside in mild regions or sheltered sites
✿	Plants that need protection from frost over winter

Mini herb garden

Perfect for beginners, herbs are resilient, can be picked over a long season, and are always useful in the kitchen. This pair of coordinating terracotta pots is filled largely with evergreen herbs that will produce aromatic leaves year after year. It makes sense to grow parsley in a separate pot, because it runs to seed in its second year and will need replacing. For a bold display choose cultivars with golden and variegated foliage, and combine them with the summer flowers of thyme, marjoram, sage, and chives, together with trailing bedding, such as petunias and brachyscome (*as shown*).

Golden marjoram
❀❀❀ ◊ ☼

Curly parsley
❀❀❀ ◊ ◐ ☼ ☼

Container basics

Size Large pot at least 25cm (10in) in diameter, small pot about 15cm (6in) in diameter
Suits Area close to the kitchen
Soil Multipurpose compost or soil-based compost, eg, John Innes No 2
Site Full sun

Shopping list

- 1 x golden marjoram
- 1 x curly parsley
- 1 x variegated sage
- 1 x bay
- 1 x chives
- 1 x golden lemon thyme

Variegated sage
❀❀❀ ◊ ☼

Bay
❀❀❀ ◊ ☼

Planting and aftercare

Herbs can be planted in spring, but if using tender bedding, wait until after the frosts. Ensure the pots have drainage holes in the base and fill with a layer of compost. Plant the thyme and flowers through the holes in the large pot, add more compost and plant the other herbs on top (*see p.59*). Plant up the smaller pot with parsley and flowers. Keep the compost just moist during the summer and water sparingly in winter. Once established, pick the leaves as required. Replant the herbs in the large container into bigger pots every two years.

Chives
❀❀❀ ◊ ◐ ☼ ☼

Golden lemon thyme
❀❀❀ ◐ ☼

Ornamental potager

Large planters, such as this rustic timber manger, offer scope for mingling flowers with vegetables to create a tiny kitchen garden or "potager". Packed with an abundance of crops that are harvested from early summer into autumn, this group also includes vibrant French marigolds for an injection of colour. Slow-growing leeks and celeriac will take time to fill the front of the bed, so make use of the spare soil by sowing a row of quick-cropping radishes between them. Bushy French beans and peas scrambling up sticks will quickly bulk out and bring height to the back of the display.

Container basics

Size Manger 85cm x 1.2m (35in x 48in)
Suits A patio or courtyard where extra height is needed
Soil Multipurpose compost
Site Full sun, sheltered from strong winds

Shopping list

- 3 x celeriac
- 2 x French marigolds (*Tagetes*)
- 7 x dwarf French bean 'Andante'
- 15 x pea 'Kelvedon Wonder'
- 25 x radish 'Mirabeau'
- 7 x leeks

Planting and aftercare

When the frosts are over, fill the manger up to 8cm (3in) below the rim with compost. Sow a row of peas at the back and add branched sticks for support. Work forward, sowing a row of French beans, and then planting a line of young leeks (*see p.55*). Plant celeriac at the front, and sow radishes between them and the leeks. Finish with French marigolds in each corner. Water well, and keep the compost moist. Once established, feed leeks and celeriac fortnightly with a balanced fertilizer, and apply tomato fertilizer weekly to the beans and peas when flowers appear.

Celeriac
❄❄ ◗ ☼

French marigold (*Tagetes*)
❄ ◊ ☼

Dwarf French bean 'Andante'
❄ ◊ ◗ ☼

Pea 'Kelvedon Wonder'
❄❄ ◊ ◗ ☼

Radish 'Mirabeau'
❄❄ ◊ ◗ ☼ ☼

Leek
❄❄❄ ◊ ☼

Mediterranean mix

Transform any warm, sunny corner with this exuberant mix of fruiting vegetable crops and flowers. Tomatoes will quickly grow up supporting canes or cascade over the sides of pots to fill the space with lush foliage, clusters of bright yellow flowers, and tempting trusses of fruits. This recipe includes a diverse range of tomato cultivars, teaming a striped 'Tigerella' with the cherry tomato 'Conchita', and intensely sweet orange-yellow 'Sungold'. Aubergines thrive in similar conditions and their silvery foliage, mauve flowers and glossy fruits look pretty in pots. Complete the composition with a flourish of fiery orange marigolds.

Pot marigold (*Calendula*)
❀ ❀ ❀ ⬦ ☼

Aubergine
❀ ⬦ ☼

Container basics

Size Pots with minimum diameter of 25cm (10in) for tomatoes and aubergine; pot 15cm (6in) in diameter for marigolds
Suits A sun-baked patio or balcony, or a conservatory or greenhouse
Soil Multipurpose compost
Site Warm, with full sun and shelter from wind

Shopping list

- 1 x pot marigold (*Calendula*)
- 1 x aubergine
- 1 x tomato 'Sungold'
- 1 x tomato 'Tigerella'
- 1 x tomato 'Conchita'

Planting and aftercare

Harden off young tomato and aubergine plants in late spring (*see p.36*) and plant out once the risk of frost is over. Check pots have drainage holes, and plant the tomatoes (*see p.51 for steps*). Plant the aubergine and marigolds at the same level as they were in their original pots. Once planted, add canes to support tall tomatoes and raise up pots planted with trailing types. Water plants consistently, never allowing the compost to dry out, and feed at least weekly with a tomato fertilizer once the first fruits appear.

Tomato 'Tigerella'
❀ ⬦ ☼

Tomato 'Sungold'
❀ ⬦ ☼

Tomato 'Conchita'
❀ ⬦ ☼

Mixed salads

Quick and easy, these colourful salad leaves, herbs, and edible flowers will be ready to pick just six weeks after sowing. Purple and pale green lettuces, sown in bands across the metal tub, rapidly fill out to form a mass of scalloped foliage, while the basket, edged with frilly 'Black Seeded Simpson' lettuce and mustard, is set off with a spray of edible marigolds. Variegated lemon thyme adds both colour and fragrance to the third pot, where feathery *Cosmos* will supply daisy-like flowers later in summer. Pick individual leaves from across the display, and these pots will keep cropping for weeks.

Container basics

Size Rustic containers about 20cm x 45cm (8in x 18in)
Suits On a patio or in a gravel garden
Soil Multipurpose compost
Site Full sun or part shade

Shopping list

- 1 x packet lettuce 'Dazzle' seed
- 1 x packet lettuce 'Green Frills' seed
- 1 x packet lettuce 'Black Seeded Simpson' seed
- 2 x pot marigolds (*Calendula*)
- 1 x packet mustard 'Red Giant' seed
- 1 x lemon thyme
- 3 x *Cosmos* (*optional*)

Planting and aftercare

Line the basket with durable plastic and make sure all pots have drainage holes. From mid-spring, fill them to about 5cm (2in) below the rim with compost and plant the thyme and marigolds in their chosen positions (plant *Cosmos* after the frosts). Level the compost surface and thinly sow 'Black Seeded Simpson' and mustard seed. Mark out diagonal bands in the metal tub and thinly sow the two lettuce cultivars so they do not mix. Cover seeds lightly with sieved compost and water. Keep well watered to prevent the salad plants rapidly running to seed.

Lettuce 'Dazzle'
❄ ◌ ◗ ☼ ☀

Lettuce 'Green Frills'
❄ ◌ ◗ ☼ ☀

Lettuce 'Black Seeded Simpson'
❄ ◌ ◗ ☼ ☀

Pot marigold (*Calendula*)
❄❄❄ ◌ ☼

Mustard 'Red Giant'
❄❄ ◌ ☼

Lemon thyme
❄❄❄ ◌ ☼

Pepper pots

Spice up a sunny patio or balcony with a colourful collection of chillies and sweet peppers. These bushy plants make attractive specimens for containers with their small white flowers followed by shiny green fruits which, depending on the cultivar, ripen to brilliant shades of yellow, orange, red, and purple. Complement these jewel colours with pots in sizzling orange, cool blue, and warm terracotta. Zesty golden marjoram and trailing *Erigeron karvinskianus*, with its pretty pink and white daisies that decorate the plant throughout the summer, make perfect partners for peppers, since they thrive in the same well-drained compost and sunny site.

Container basics

Size Pots at least 20cm (8in) in diameter
Suits Sheltered patios or balconies, or in a conservatory or greenhouse
Soil Multipurpose or soil-based compost, eg, John Innes No 2
Site Full sun indoors or outside

Shopping list

- 1 x chilli pepper 'Numex Twilight'
- 1 x chilli pepper 'Fresno'
- 1 x sweet pepper 'Sweet Banana'
- 1 x *Erigeron karvinskianus*
- 1 x golden marjoram

Planting and aftercare

Harden off pepper and chilli plants gradually and plant outside after the frosts (*see p.36*), or grow indoors. Check pots have drainage holes, and cover them with a layer of broken pot pieces, followed by some compost. Plant a pepper or chilli plant in the centre of each pot, ensuring that it is planted at the same depth as in its original pot. Firm in, and water (*see also p.50*). Water when the compost surface dries out and feed fortnightly with tomato fertilizer when fruits appear. Tie fruit-laden plants to canes for support.

Chilli pepper 'Fresno'
❄ ◌ ☼

Chilli pepper 'Numex Twilight'
❄ ◌ ☼

Sweet pepper 'Sweet Banana'
❄ ◌ ☼

Erigeron karvinskianus
❄❄❄ ◌ ☼

Golden marjoram
❄❄❄ ◌ ☼

Tomato and herb basket

You can squeeze extra growing space into small plots and onto patios with a hanging basket or two. While they are more commonly used for bedding plants, a collection of vegetables, herbs, and edible flowers offers an equally stunning display. Choose a large, deep basket that provides plenty of space for these vigorous plants to grow. Team hot red nasturtiums and cherry tomatoes with purple stems of cinnamon basil and cool blue violas. If well fed and watered, this basket will look great throughout summer and provide a plentiful harvest.

Tomato 'Tumbler'
❄ ◊ ☼

Chives
❄❄❄ ◊ ◐ ☼ ☀

Container basics

Size Basket at least 30cm (12in) in diameter
Suits Walls, fences, and sheds within easy reach for picking
Soil Multipurpose compost
Site Full sun, sheltered from wind

Shopping list

- 2 x tomato 'Tumbler'
- 2 x chives
- 2 x parsley 'Moss Curled'
- 2 x viola
- 2 x nasturtium (*Tropaeolum*) 'Empress of India'
- 1 x cinnamon basil

Parsley 'Moss Curled'
❄❄❄ ◊ ◐ ☼ ☀

Blue viola
❄❄❄ ◊ ◐ ☼ ☀

Planting and aftercare

Basil, tomatoes, and nasturtiums cannot tolerate cold conditions, so plant up after the frosts. Ensure the basket is lined with plastic, and pierce it to allow free drainage. Fill the base with multipurpose compost and mix in water-retaining crystals if desired. Find the best layout for the plants in the basket while they are still in their pots, positioning the trailing tomatoes near the edge. Water the plants well, knock them from their pots, and plant in the basket. Firm well, water, and hang on a sturdy bracket. Water daily in summer and apply a tomato feed weekly once fruits show.

Nasturtium 'Empress of India'
❄ ◊ ☼

Cinnamon basil
❄ ◊ ☼

Barbecue collection

As well the being the perfect place for a barbecue, a sunny patio is also the best spot for these containers filled with summer vegetables ideal for the grill. A single courgette plant creates instant impact with its huge leaves and golden flowers, and can deliver as many as 20 plump fruits over many weeks. Vigorous nasturtiums (*Tropaeolum*) will happily scramble among the foliage, sending out flushes of glowing red edible flowers that can be used in salads. Sweetcorn makes an exotic backdrop and the sweetest, freshly picked cobs are a real treat when cooked over coals. Also grow a sweet pepper in a neighbouring pot to complete the display.

Container basics

Size Two pots at least 60cm (2ft) and 20cm (8in) in diameter
Suits Patio or dining area
Soil Multipurpose or soil-based compost, such as John Innes No 1, mixed with well-rotted manure
Site Full sun, sheltered from wind

Shopping list

- 1 x courgette 'Safari'
- 3 x sweetcorn 'Earlybird'
- 1 x pepper 'Redskin'
- 4 x nasturtium (*Tropaeolum*) 'Red Wonder'

Planting and aftercare

Courgettes, peppers, and sweetcorn are not hardy, so wait until after the last frost to plant them outside. Fill a large pot with compost to 5cm (2in) below the rim. Water the plants, knock them from their pots and plant the sweetcorn at the back, the courgette towards the front (*see also pp.52–53*), and the nasturtiums in between. Plant the pepper separately in a smaller pot (*see p.50*). Water in well. Don't allow the compost to dry out, and feed plants at least weekly with a tomato fertilizer when the first fruits form.

Courgette 'Safari'
❄ ◌ ☼

Sweetcorn 'Earlybird'
❄ ◌ ☼

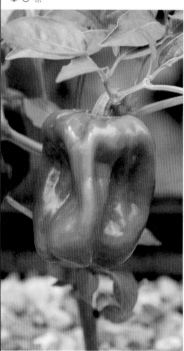

Pepper 'Redskin'
❄ ◌ ☼

Nasturtium 'Red Wonder'
❄❄❄ ◌ ☼

Tempting roots

Vintage wooden crates, weathered terracotta pots, and an old hessian bag combine to form a shabby chic collection of containers for easy-to-grow root crops. Burgundy-stemmed beetroot leaves and feathery carrot foliage offer a textural contrast in the two crates, while vivid magenta dwarf *Cosmos* picks up the colour of the beetroot. The potatoes produce a mass of dark green foliage to set off the display and a bag full of tubers come early summer.

Container basics

Size Wooden crates 50cm x 20cm (20in x 8in); terracotta pot 15cm (6in) in diameter; large hessian bag
Suits An informal space with a cottage-garden style
Soil Multipurpose or soil-based compost
Site Full sun, sheltered from wind

Shopping list

- 3 x *Cosmos bipinnatus* 'Sonata' plants
- 1 x packet beetroot 'Boltardy' seeds
- 1 x packet carrot 'Resistafly'
- 3 x seed potatoes, eg, 'Kestrel'

Planting and aftercare

Chit the seed potatoes in early spring (*see p.43 for planting steps*). Line the crates and bag with plastic and pierce with a kitchen fork to create holes for drainage. In mid-spring fill the crates with compost up to 5cm (2in) below the top, and thinly sow the carrot and beetroot seeds. Cover with a thin layer of compost and water well. Fill the bag one-third full with compost, plant the potatoes and cover with 15cm (6in) of compost. Water well. When the beetroot and carrot seedlings appear, thin to the distances given on the seed packs, or a little closer. Also add compost to "earth up" the potatoes as they grow. Plant the *Cosmos* in their pot once the risk of frost is over. Water regularly, and apply a balanced liquid fertilizer every fortnight.

Cosmos bipinnatus 'Sonata'
❄ ◊ ◗ ☼

Beetroot 'Boltardy'
❄❄❄ ◊ ☼

Carrot 'Resistafly'
❄❄❄ ◊ ☼

Potato 'Kestrel'
❄ ◊ ◗ ☼

Bean feast

Pack a group of beans into your plot with bushy dwarf cultivars that are perfectly suited to pots, and vigorous climbing types trained neatly up canes or trellis. Here, the scarlet flowers and long runner beans of 'Enorma' make a bold backdrop alongside mottled pink borlotti beans. The dwarf French bean 'Pencil Pod Black Wax' produces slender pods after the mauve flowers, while the compact runner bean 'Hestia', nasturtiums (*Tropaeolum*), marigolds, and lobelia offer more colour.

Container basics

Size Containers at least 45cm (18in) in diameter for beans; pots 15cm (6in) in diameter for the flowers
Suits Corners of patios and terraces
Soil Multipurpose or soil-based compost
Site Full sun, sheltered from wind

Shopping list

- 5 x runner bean 'Enorma'
- 4 x dwarf French bean 'Pencil Pod Black Wax'
- 3 x runner bean 'Hestia'
- 5 x borlotti bean 'Borlotto Lingua di Fuoco'
- 2 x nasturtium (*Tropaeolum*) 'Peach Melba Superior'
- 3 x French marigolds (*Tagetes*)

Planting and aftercare

Sow beans indoors from early to mid-spring, in their final positions in late spring, or buy young plants. Acclimatize plants to outdoor conditions before planting (*see p.36*). Check containers have drainage holes and fill with compost up to 5cm (2in) below the rim. Erect canes for climbing beans and plant at the base of each cane (*see also pp.48–49*). Allow about 20cm (8in) between dwarf beans and add supports to prop them up when laden with beans. Water well and tie-in climbing beans. Water consistently and feed weekly with a tomato fertilizer when flowers appear.

Runner bean 'Enorma'
❄ ◌ ◗ ☀

French bean 'Pencil Pod Black Wax'
❄ ◌ ◗ ☀

Runner bean 'Hestia'
❄ ◌ ◗ ☀

Bean 'Borlotto Lingua di Fuoco'
❄ ◌ ◗ ☀

Nasturtium 'Peach Melba Superior'
❄ ❄ ❄ ◌ ☀

French marigold (*Tagetes*)
❄ ◌ ☀

Refreshing mints

Always in demand in the kitchen, mint is valuable in the garden too because it flourishes in shady conditions which don't suit most herbs. Take advantage of the diversity of sizes, foliage colours, and subtle scents and tastes of different types of mint, and set pots close to the kitchen. Easy to grow and perennial, mint is also invasive and best grown on its own, as it will quickly swamp other plants. Here, lush green garden, basil, and Morrocan mints complement the warm terracotta tones of the pots, while the pale variegation of the pineapple mint creates a lively contrast to dark purple petunias and dainty violas.

Container basics

Size Two pots at least 25cm (10in) in diameter
Suits Any space handy for picking
Soil Multipurpose or soil-based compost
Site A patio or balcony in semi-shade

Shopping list

- 1 x garden mint (spearmint)
- 1 x *Petunia* 'Phantom'
- 1 x viola
- 1 x Moroccan mint
- 1 x basil mint
- 1 x pineapple mint

Planting and aftercare

Mints are best planted in spring, but petunias are killed by frost, so plant this display in late spring or early summer. Ensure the containers have drainage holes; the tall chimney pot used here has a plastic pot slotted into it. Fill the base of each pot with a layer of compost, and arrange the plants in their best positions in the containers. Then water them well, knock them from their pots, and plant up. Firm the compost and water in well. Keep the mints moist throughout the growing season, cut back old stems when they die down in winter, and apply an all-purpose granular fertilizer in spring.

Garden mint (spearmint)
❄❄❄ ◐ ☼ ☼

Petunia 'Phantom'
❄ ◌ ◐ ☼

Viola
❄❄❄ ◌ ◐ ☼ ☼

Moroccan mint
❄❄❄ ◐ ☼ ☼

Basil mint
❄❄❄ ◐ ☼ ☼

Pineapple mint
❄❄❄ ◐ ☼ ☼

Beautiful berries

Combine a range of summer berries in large containers to create a beautiful display of stems, leaves, flowers, and fruits in succession throughout the year. Choose a variety of fruits for a sweet harvest right through summer and select compact cultivars that are suitable for growing in pots. This combination of an unusual red-fruited gooseberry, thornless blackberry with decorative double pink flowers, and two different blueberry cultivars to ensure a good crop, would look great on any patio or balcony. Boost the summer colour as the fruits ripen with bedding plants, such as *Torenia*.

Container basics

Size Large pots at least 30cm (12in) in diameter
Suits An area convenient for picking
Soil Ericaceous compost for blueberries, soil-based compost, such as John Innes No 2, for other fruit bushes
Site Full sun

Shopping list

- 1 x blueberry 'Patriot'
- 1 x blueberry 'Bluecrop'
- 1 x blackberry 'Loch Maree'
- 3 x *Torenia* plants
- 1 x gooseberry 'Hinnomaki Red'

Planting and aftercare

Select four large containers with drainage holes in their bases. Plant the gooseberry and blackberry in separate pots filled with soil-based compost. Take care not to bury plants any deeper than they were planted in their original pots. Plant the blueberries in ericaceous compost (*see also pp.60–63 for more details*). When there is no risk of frost, plant the *Torenia* around the fruit bushes. Keep pots well watered. Apply an all-purpose granular fertilizer in spring to the blackberries and gooseberries, and a slow-release fertilizer for ericaceous plants to the blueberries. Repot all fruit bushes every two years.

Blueberry 'Patriot'
❋❋❋ ◑ ☼

Blueberry 'Bluecrop'
❋❋❋ ◑ ☼

Blackberry 'Loch Maree'
❋❋❋ ◑ ☼ ☀

Torenia
❋ ◌ ◑ ☼ ☀

Gooseberry 'Hinnomaki Red'
❋❋❋ ◑ ☼ ☀

Caring for your crops

Plants in containers can't sink their roots deep into the soil to seek out water and nutrients, and instead rely on you to look after their needs. To help you to care for your crops, this chapter outlines all the essential techniques needed to keep your plants healthy and productive. Discover the most effective ways to water and feed crops at various stages of their development, and how to keep your pots weed free. There are also tips on harvesting and storing your produce, protecting tender plants from frost, and repotting fruit trees to provide space for them to mature. Making your own garden compost is another useful skill to learn, as it provides plants with essential nutrients and is a fantastic soil conditioner. Finally, there's guidance on pests and diseases, with a gallery of common types to help you diagnose and deal with any problems that arise.

Feeding, weeding, and watering

Crops grown in pots need extra care because they can't sink their roots deep into the soil to tap into the nutrients and moisture there. Daily watering and regular feeding are essential, but weeds should not be a serious problem.

Feeding

Fresh compost contains all the essential nutrients plants need to grow and establish, but when they become exhausted, most crops will need extra fertilizer. Quick-growing salads and roots should not need feeding, while peas and beans are able take nitrogen, needed for healthy leaves, from the air, but require fertilizers rich in potassium (potash) to develop an abundance of flowers and pods. Many fruiting vegetables, such as tomatoes, courgettes, and squashes, also require regular applications of potassium fertilizer, such as tomato food, once their first fruits have set to sustain further flowering and fruiting.

Long-lived crops Feed leafy crops, such as chard and kale, every few weeks with a nitrogen-rich fertilizer. However, nitrogen promotes soft new growth, which draws pests and can be damaged by frost, so use sparingly and don't apply in autumn. Top-dress fruit trees and bushes in spring with a slow-release, granular all-purpose fertilizer, which contains a balance of all the main plant nutrients.

Liquid fertilizers come in concentrated or ready-to-use forms, and are easy to apply as part of your regular watering routine.

Dry fertilizers are available as granules or pellets. Add them to pots in spring to give perennial plants a nutrient boost.

Weeding

One huge advantage that container gardening has over growing crops in a conventional plot is that weeds are less prolific and easily controlled. Unlike garden soil, most commercially produced compost is free of weed seeds, which means that vegetable seeds should be the only plants that germinate in your pots. Of course weed seeds will blow in and could be present in any home-made compost, so watch out for their seedlings and pluck them out with your fingers as soon as you see them.

Large, perennial weeds Dandelions and other weeds with long tap roots can be lifted from the compost with a hand fork. Check your containers regularly for these pernicious weeds because they can be difficult to remove once their roots become entwined with those of your crops. Be sure to remove all weeds before they flower and start producing seeds of their own.

Dandelions and many other perennial weeds regrow from tiny root sections, so remove all plant parts carefully.

Watering

Watering not only prevents wilting but also allows plants to take up soluble nutrients in the compost. The task requires careful judgement to ensure that established plants have enough moisture to sustain them, and that seedlings and young plants are not over-watered. You may need to water twice a day in hot weather, and check containers regularly, even after rain, because plants' foliage often prevents moisture reaching the compost. To make the job easier, invest in quality watering cans, or install a hose or irrigation system for larger collections of pots.

After sowing seed, soak the compost and allow to drain, either by placing the pots in trays of water until the compost surface feels moist, or by watering from above using a can fitted with a fine rose. Both methods avoid disturbing the seeds. Strips of moisture-retentive felted material (*above*) also help to keep seed trays moist.

Use a fine rose when watering with a can to create a gentle shower of water that will be absorbed gradually, rather than a single gush from a spout which simply runs off the surface, displacing compost and uncovering plant roots. The most efficient times to water are early in the morning or in the evening when evaporation rates are low.

Trees in containers require large amounts of water to remain healthy and produce fruits. Soak pots so that water fills the area between the compost and the rim, either using a hose on a gentle spray setting or a watering can with a rose. Top the pot with a thick mulch of gravel to prevent water loss and stop compost washing away.

An automatic irrigation system is a good investment if you have lots of pots, or work and holidays make watering by hand impossible. Water flows through a hose to drip feeders placed in containers; the hose is attached to a timer which turns the system on and off. Select a system that suits your needs and is easy to set up.

Making your own compost

Make the most of a quiet corner of your garden with a compost bin, and turn kitchen peelings and garden waste into valuable compost for free. There are bins to fit plots of every size and style, and the rich compost they generate can be used to give your productive pots a nutrient boost year after year.

Choosing a compost bin

There is an enormous range of compost bins on offer, and where space is limited it is important to choose one that looks good and suits your garden style. The essential requirements are an open base, a lid or cover, and good access to turn the heap and remove the finished product. Also try to match the size of the bin to the amount of organic waste generated from your garden and kitchen. Plastic bins are economical and long-lasting, while wooden containers look more appealing and are a good choice if your bin will be on view. Alternatively, you could build your own made-to-measure timber bin.

Filling your bin

Find a suitable site in full sun or part shade for your compost heap. Also place the bin on soil rather than a paved surface to provide access for creatures that help the composting process. Try to achieve an equal balance of nitrogen-rich green material, such as spent vegetable plants and kitchen peelings, and drier carbon-rich waste, like dead leaves, small twigs, and shredded paper. Avoid composting cooked foods, which can attract vermin. Mix different types of waste, rather than creating thick layers, as this allows moisture and air to circulate more freely. Also add water if the heap looks too dry.

Turning the compost

Waste breaks down faster in the warm, damp conditions at the centre of a compost heap than it does at the cool, dry edges, so for all the material in the heap to break down evenly it needs to be turned. Wait until the bin is full and then lift the contents out of the bin onto the soil or a tarpaulin, mix them together, and then put them back again. Alternatively, if you have space for two bins, simply turn the heap from one into the other using a garden fork. Once the material in your bin has been turned do not add more waste; crumbly compost with an earthy smell should then be ready in a few months.

Other forms of compost

Using wormeries

Wormeries are a good option for small gardens where there is less waste to compost. They employ large numbers of special composting worms to break down organic matter into a fine, fertile soil improver that's perfect for productive pots. Specially designed plastic containers with good drainage and ventilation are available to house the worms. They can be placed in a garage or outside in summer but need to be insulated from frost in winter. It's best to start a wormery in spring or summer, when the worms will breed rapidly and establish quickly. Feed them well with leafy garden waste, kitchen scraps (not meat or fish), and shredded newspaper.

Making leafmould

Fallen autumn leaves are a valuable resource because they break down to form dark, crumbly leafmould, which is an excellent soil improver for containers and raised beds. Leafmould is easy to make, by gathering up damp leaves and placing them in a plastic sack. Tie the top, pierce the bag a few times with a garden fork, and place it somewhere shady and out of the way for up to two years while the leaves decompose. Fill a few bags if you have plenty of leaves, as each one will produce just enough leafmould for two or three pots when mixed with compost. The fact that leaves break down slowly means they are best kept separate from the main compost heap.

Bokashi composting

This technique works by introducing micro-organisms to ferment kitchen and soft garden waste in a small, airtight caddy. The process does not produce odours and the sealed container keeps flies away from the waste, making bokashi a good option for indoor composting. Simply add organic material, including meat, fish, and dairy waste, to the caddy and scatter with wheat bran that has been inoculated with bokashi micro-organisms. Continue until the caddy is full and the fermentation will be complete in about two weeks. The appearance of the waste changes little, but it is a good nutrient source when buried in compost and the liquid produced can be diluted at a rate of 1:100 parts water and used as fertilizer.

Harvesting and storing

Picking crops at the right moment guarantees the best flavour and means your produce is in perfect condition for storing. You can then use a few easy methods to preserve that just-picked taste for delicious treats all year.

Picking fruit

Recognising when fruit is ready to pick is an important skill. Most soft fruits take on a rich, deep colour and have glossy skin when ripe. If they look dull and puckered it usually means that they have been left on the plant for too long. This is also true of cherries, which should be cut together with their stalks using scissors. Apples, plums, peaches, nectarines, and apricots are usually picked when fully ripe, and should come away easily in your hand. Pears and late apples finish ripening off the tree; give the fruits a sharp twist to pull them off with their stalks. If in doubt, taste fruit before harvesting the whole crop and pick carefully to avoid bruising, which spoils the taste and storage potential.

Picking early to mid-season apples in late summer and autumn is a real pleasure. Gently lift and twist the fruits and if ripe they will part from the tree easily.

Harvesting vegetables

Many vegetables are ripe for picking when young and tender, and if left too long can become starchy and tough. Check crops every day during summer to catch them at the peak of perfection. Plucking fast-growing peas, beans, and courgettes when they are small and tender not only gives you the sweetest vegetables but it also stimulates the plant into producing more crops. Potatoes are usually ready to harvest once they begin flowering, while other roots, like radishes and beetroots, are best pulled when small to prevent them becoming woody. Most fruiting vegetables develop the finest flavour when left to mature on the plant, but pick sweetcorn as soon as the silky tassels turn brown, or cobs will lose their sweet juiciness.

Pick courgettes frequently to enjoy them while the flesh is dense and full-flavoured, because they rapidly balloon into watery marrows. Cut through the stout stem of the fruit with a clean, sharp knife.

Drying and curing

A number of vegetable crops will store well in a cool, frost-free place if their skins are allowed to dry out or cure in the sun during late summer or autumn. This simple process works well for winter squashes, onions, shallots, and garlic, which do not have to be used immediately after harvesting. Lift garlic from the soil as its leaves yellow and allow the foliage of onions and shallots to die down naturally before lifting them from their containers, taking care not to bruise the bulbs. Spread them out on wire mesh for 7 to 10 days in the sunshine, or indoors if it is wet. Leave winter squashes on the plant to mature, then cut the stems, leaving them as long as possible, and set the fruits in the sun for 10 days. This toughens the skin so that the fruits will keep for many months, providing a delicious ingredient for winter recipes.

Colourful winter squashes develop hard skins when left to cure in the sun; the tougher the skin the more water they will retain, thereby prolonging their shelf life.

Freezing and preserving

Quick and easy, these simple methods of squirrelling away excess harvests are well worth trying. Large quantities of produce are not necessary to make storing worthwhile; it's really satisfying to make homemade chutney or freeze berries for a winter pudding, bringing those summery tastes to the table in the depths of the coldest season. Almost all fruit and vegetables can be stored in some way, so there's no need to waste any crops. Remember to sterilize glass preserving jars before use by washing in hot, soapy water and drying thoroughly in a moderate oven.

Beetroot relish is just one of many relishes, pickles, and chutneys that can be made by cooking produce in water, sugar, and vinegar and storing in sterilized jars. Look for recipes in books and online to make the most of your favourite crops.

Homemade pesto is easy to make by combining herbs, pine nuts, garlic, oil, and Parmesan cheese. Try using other abundant spicy leaf crops like rocket as interesting alternatives to traditional basil, and store under a layer of oil in jars in the fridge.

Freezing fruit is the quickest way to keep berries (except strawberries), currants, and apples for winter. Lay soft fruit on a tray, freeze, and then store in bags. Stew apples and allow to cool before freezing. Alternatively, use berries to make jam.

Protecting tender plants

Protecting fruit and vegetable plants from the damaging effects of frost allows tender crops to be grown in cooler climates, and many hardier types to be sown earlier and harvested later, greatly extending the cropping season.

Temporary frost protection

Plants in containers are easy to protect on unexpectedly cold nights in spring or autumn. Small pots can be moved indoors, while covering crops in larger containers is an effective way to prevent damage. Half-hardy crops, such as tomatoes, peppers, courgettes, and runner beans, are particularly vulnerable to frost damage, even when acclimatized to outdoor conditions, and need protection. It is also worth covering many early spring sowings and leafy autumn crops to improve their performance.

Cloches and horticultural fleece Designed to keep out the cold, traditional cloches are made of glass, but plastic alternatives are easier to use and safer for crops in containers. Bell-shaped designs are suitable for covering a pot full of young plants, while longer tunnels are useful for raised beds and growing tables. Sheets or tubes of horticultural fleece will protect plants of any size; either support it on wires or canes, or just drape it over plants.

Wrap tender plants with horticultural fleece if frost threatens. Cover the plant loosely and tie securely to the pot with twine to stop it blowing away.

All citrus trees, including tangerines (*above*), must be overwintered in a cool room indoors with plenty of daylight to encourage the fruits to form and ripen.

Overwintering tender plants

Most fruit and vegetables that are not hardy are grown each year from seed as annual summer crops. However, it is worth overwintering citrus trees and chilli plants indoors, not only because they won't tolerate the cold, but also because they produce welcome fruits in winter. Bring plants in before the first frost and place them in a bright room, such as a cool conservatory or porch.

Providing suitable conditions Centrally heated houses can prove challenging because these plants don't enjoy hot, dry air. Place them in a relatively cool room, away from radiators and draughts; remember too that windowsills will be too cold at night in winter for many tender crops. Increase the humidity by placing pots on dishes or trays filled with gravel and water. Water plants sparingly and do not feed chillies during winter as they do not grow strongly in low light levels. Apply a winter citrus fertilizer fortnightly to the citrus trees (*see also pp.66–67*).

Repotting fruit trees

Sustaining healthy growth

All fruit trees will need repotting to give their roots space to grow and to provide them with fresh, nutrient-rich compost. Trees that are in the process of growing to their final size should be moved into a larger container every year, while mature specimens need repotting every couple of years. It's best to do this in late autumn, but you can repot your trees at any time while they are dormant from winter until early spring, weather permitting.

1 Gently knock the plant from its pot. Larger trees may need to be laid down carefully and pulled by the trunk; ask someone to help you if the pot and root ball are heavy.

2 While holding the trunk to prevent damaging the branches, carefully tease out the roots around the edge of the root ball. Remove some of the old compost as you go.

3 To help prevent the tree becoming pot bound, trim the roots using secateurs. Select long, thick roots and any that have been damaged; remove using a clean, angled cut.

4 Choose a new pot slightly larger than the old one and check that it has drainage holes. Use fresh, soil-based compost and plant so that it reaches the old soil mark on the trunk. Firm, water well, and apply a mulch if desired.

Dealing with pests

Your garden will never be completely free of pests, but damage can be limited by creating barriers to keep them at bay and encouraging beneficial wildlife that feeds on them. Strong, healthy plants are more able to shrug off pest attacks than weak ones, so feeding and watering your crops pay dividends too.

Catch problems early Check plants frequently for the first signs of a pest attack, as small numbers are easier to deal with and rarely cause serious damage. However, some insect pests are hard to spot, so also look out for leaf damage or curling, droppings, and sticky honeydew on foliage. For common pests, such as slugs and carrot flies, it's best to assume that they will target your crops and to take preventative measures, because by the time you see the damage your crops may be beyond repair.

Prevent attacks Try planting flowers alongside crops to attract beneficial insects, such as lacewings, that prey on pests. Remember that pesticides may kill beneficial insects as well as villains, so use them carefully and always follow the instructions. Barriers, such as fleece and netting, will effectively keep pests and plants apart, while sticky sheets in the greenhouse can help to reduce pest numbers. Biological controls are also effective when used correctly. In addition, buy pest-resistant cultivars and reduce soil-borne pest numbers by using fresh compost in your pots.

Use sticky plastic sheets in the greenhouse to trap flying pests.

Copper tape fixed around cloches or pots helps to deter slugs and snails. The copper reacts with their slime to give them an uncomfortable electric shock that stops them in their tracks.

Netting prevents hungry birds and insects devouring fruit crops. Support it with canes so that it doesn't damage the plants, and weigh it down at the base to prevent it blowing away.

Barriers can prevent damage from flying insects, such as carrot fly. This pest flies close to the ground so a pot and barrier that together measure 60cm (2ft) high will prevent attacks.

Pest predators

Many common creatures prey on the pests that attack fruit and vegetable plants and they can be encouraged into the garden to help protect your crops. The key is to cater to the needs of these beneficial creatures year-round. Undisturbed spaces between containers provide shady places for wildlife to hide, while growing a variety of flowering plants alongside your fruit and vegetables not only looks attractive but also attracts pest predators, such as hoverflies and lacewings. Even a small source of water will lure birds, frogs, and hedgehogs, which all help to keep pests at bay, and grow plants up walls and fences to provide them with cover. Also try to include evergreen shrubs for insects to overwinter in and pile up autumn leaves to provide small creatures with a home.

Ladybird larvae are not as pretty as the adults, but an insatiable appetite for aphids and other insect pests and their eggs makes these small, black, orange-striped beasts welcome visitors.

Ladybirds love nothing better than feasting on aphids. Nurture a healthy population in your garden by providing a good variety of dry places for them to gather and overwinter.

Song thrushes eat snails by cracking their shells on large stones, so place a few around the garden. Also provide them with berry-bearing shrubs in winter when insects are scarce.

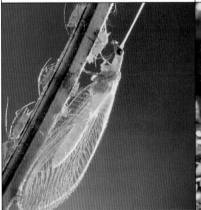

Lacewings and their larvae are valuable allies that feast on aphids and other insect pests. Lure them into the garden with a range of nectar-rich flowers that bloom at different times.

Frogs and toads like damp and shady nooks and crannies to hide in during the day, and some water for breeding in spring. In return, they will hunt for your slugs in the cool of the night.

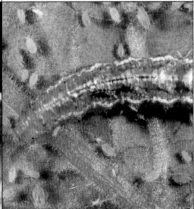

Hoverfly larvae can consume hundreds of aphids before they pupate, so attract the adults with flowering plants and they will repay you by laying their eggs in your garden.

Common pests

Whitefly
Plants grown under cover are particularly susceptible to attack from these small, sap-sucking, white-winged insects. Watch out for the sticky honeydew that they secrete on leaves, and adult flies taking flight when plants are disturbed. Treat with the biological control *Encarsia formosa* from mid-spring to mid-autumn.

Red spider mite
Mottled, dull leaves on fruit trees and plants grown in a greenhouse are a sign of red spider mite infestation. Check the underside of leaves for tiny green mites, which turn red in autumn, and fine silk webbing. Keep humidity high in hot weather and use the biological control *Phytoseiulus persimilis,* or try fatty acid sprays.

Slugs and snails
Slimy trails, irregular holes in leaves and decimated seedlings are all signs of these pests. They can be controlled by collecting them by torchlight at night, finding the areas where they gather to overwinter, wrapping copper tape around pots, sparing use of slug pellets, or using a nematode biological control in spring or autumn.

Carrot fly
Female carrot flies lay eggs on the soil surface between late spring and early autumn, and the small, cream larvae then tunnel into the roots causing unsightly brown lines. Prevent the low-flying females from reaching crops by growing carrots under fleece or in tall pots, erecting barriers, or sowing resistant cultivars.

Capsid bug
Leaves at the shoot tips of many plants, including currants, become deformed and peppered with small holes when these small, pale green insects feed on their sap. Apple capsid bugs also feed on young fruits, which develop raised patches that only affect the skin. Taste is not affected so control is not necessary.

Aphids
Often found on tender new shoots, these sap-feeding insects include greenfly and blackfly. Healthy plants can usually tolerate small numbers, but aphids can distort new growth and transmit viruses. Control them by squashing them, encouraging natural predators (*see p.103*), or spraying them with pyrethrum or fatty acids.

Birds

Opportunists, birds can damage foliage, eat fruit and pull up seedlings and sets when feeding in the soil. Rather than attempting to keep them out of the garden, the best way to prevent damage is to cover susceptible pots with netting that is well secured at the base to prevent birds becoming tangled in it.

Mice

Often unseen, these small mammals can cause considerable damage. They have a taste for recently sown pea, bean, and sweetcorn seeds, and can strip pods and cobs when ripe. They will also feast on stored fruit and vegetables. Set mouse traps around vulnerable crops, but cover them to safeguard pets and other animals.

Flea beetles

Small holes found in the leaves of brassicas, and rocket, radish, and pak choi, are caused by these 2–4mm (⅛–¼in) beetles. Heavy infestations can kill seedlings. Their presence is easy to spot because they leap off leaves when disturbed. Protect plants with horticultural fleece and, if necessary, control with pyrethrum.

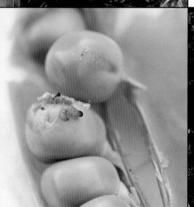

Gooseberry sawfly

Sawfly larvae defoliate gooseberries, and red and whitecurrants, from mid-spring to summer. The small green caterpillars, usually with black spots, can be difficult to spot until damage is severe, so check bushes regularly. Pick them off by hand, spray with pyrethrum or use a nematode biological control.

Pea moth

Dark-headed caterpillars feed on peas inside the pods after the female moths have laid their eggs on the flowers, leaving no sign that the peas have been spoiled. The moths lay eggs in early to midsummer, so cover peas that flower at this time with fine netting. You can also avoid attacks by sowing peas early in the season or later, when the moths are not laying.

Onion fly

Young onion plants, and occasionally leeks, shallots, and garlic, grow poorly and eventually die, as their roots are consumed by white maggots. In late summer the maggots also tunnel into onion bulbs, allowing rots to set in. Destroy all affected plants and grow onions from sets, which are less vulnerable to attack.

Dealing with diseases and disorders

Healthy plants have stronger defences against infection than those that are left wilting and malnourished, so water your crops regularly and provide them with the correct balance of nutrients to keep problems at bay.

Sterilizing seed-sowing equipment helps to prevent diseases.

Bacteria, fungi, and viruses These all cause diseases in plants and many infect weeds and dead plant material, so try to keep the garden tidy to help reduce problems. Also, avoid introducing diseases to your containers by buying certified disease-free plants and tubers, and never take cuttings or seeds from infected plants. Fungi thrive in moist, stagnant air, which is why it is vital to ventilate greenhouses and cloches, allow space between plants, and prune fruit bushes and trees. Also control pests, such as aphids, because they can spread viruses too.

Disorders Although they often look like diseases, disorders are due to other factors, such as lack of water or nutrient deficiencies. One example is blossom end rot on tomatoes, which is caused by a lack of calcium. Improving the water supply to allow better nutrient uptake is often the best remedy, or you may have to apply a fertilizer.

Clean tools after using them on individual plants.

Keep pots well watered to prevent the compost from drying out, as desiccated crops are vulnerable to diseases. Where crops, such as courgettes, are susceptible to fungal diseases, water the soil rather than the leaves.

Cut out diseased growth promptly to prevent the infection spreading, and remove any damaged growth which may provide an entry point for diseases. Cut back to the base of a leaf or to a healthy bud on a stem.

Common diseases and disorders

Damping off
Seedlings, particularly those grown under cover, are prone to this fungal disease, which causes them to collapse suddenly and die. Reduce the risk of infection by sterilizing pots and seed trays, and water seedlings with mains water. Also sow seeds thinly, provide good ventilation and apply a copper-based fungicide.

Bitter pit
Apples develop dark, sunken spots on their skins, and brown flecks on the flesh that may also have an unpleasant bitter taste. The problem can develop on the tree or in storage and is due to calcium deficiency, often caused by reduced nutrient uptake in dry conditions. Water trees regularly to protect developing fruits.

Apple and pear scabs
The skins of fruits develop dark brown, rough patches that may crack and become infected with secondary rots. Grey spots on leaves may also appear and may fall early. The fungi overwinters on fallen leaves, so pick them up in autumn, grow scab-resistant cultivars, and use fungicides for edible crops if necessary.

  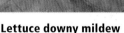

Scorch
Pale marks on leaves and flowers, which then turn dry and papery, are a sign of damage by exposure to hot or bright sunlight. Scorch can be particularly prevalent where water droplets are lying on the leaves. To prevent damage, water in the evening and ensure that greenhouse plants have adequate shading.

Blossom end rot
Pot-grown tomatoes are particularly susceptible to this problem, which is caused when dryness around the roots prevents the uptake of calcium. The bases of fruits become tough and turn from brown to black, making them inedible. Pick off affected fruits and prevent by growing in large containers and watering regularly.

Lettuce downy mildew
Older, outer leaves of lettuces develop yellow patches that turn brown, then become thin and papery or brown and soft with fluffy fungal growth. Pick off infected leaves promptly or remove the whole plant. This fungus thrives in wet, humid conditions, so give plants space to allow good air flow and ventilate greenhouses, or try resistant cultivars.

Diseases and disorders *continued*

Cucumber mosaic virus

Cucumbers, courgettes, and squashes can all catch this common disease. It causes leaves to become stunted and develop a yellow mosaic pattern, while the fruits become dark green, hard, and inedible. Control weeds, as many carry the virus, look out for aphids, which can infect plants, and grow resistant cultivars.

Powdery mildews

This fungal disease affects many fruit and vegetable plants and is easy to identify by the white, powdery fungal growth that appears on leaf surfaces. Leaves often turn yellow, growth can be poor and plants may die in extreme cases. It is worse in dry conditions, so water well, remove infected leaves, and apply fungicides if necessary.

Potato and tomato blight

This fungus affects potatoes and tomatoes, causing brown patches on leaf edges that spread and lead them to wither and die. Tubers and fruits also develop dark, sunken patches and then rot. Remove and destroy infected foliage and apply fungicides for edible crops if needed. Also lift tubers early, and grow resistant cultivars.

Rusts

Beans, leeks, and plums are among the many crops prone to various rust diseases, which cause patches of bright orange fungal spores on leaves and stems. Reduce their spread by improving air circulation between plants, remove and destroy infected material, grow resistant cultivars, and use fungicides for edible crops.

Strawberry viruses

Evidence that strawberries have been infected with a virus include distorted foliage with strange yellow markings, stunted plant growth, and poor flowering and fruiting. Dig up and destroy plants, control aphids which can spread the disease and do not replant strawberries in the same soil. Also buy certified disease-free plants.

American gooseberry mildew

This fungal disease causes powdery white patches on the leaves, stems, and fruit of gooseberries and sometimes blackcurrants. Shoot tips may die back and although fruit is still edible it does not look tempting. Prevent infection by pruning bushes to increase air-flow, and growing disease-resistant cultivars.

Peach leaf curl

This disease causes blistered leaves that turn coral-red and purple. Peach trees are most susceptible from winter to late spring; keeping them dry in a greenhouse or under a polythene shelter helps to prevent infection. Trees may recover if fed and watered well and diseased leaves removed, or treat infected plants with a fungicide.

Bean chocolate spot

Dark brown spots appear on the foliage, stems, and pods of bean plants, spreading to form large patches of infection that can reduce yields or destroy crops. The fungus responsible flourishes in damp conditions, so grow beans in well-drained soil, give them plenty of space, and keep compost weed free.

Botrytis

Common grey mould can affect most plants, usually infecting them through damaged tissue. It causes fluffy off-white or grey fungal growth on patches of brown, soft, rotting tissue, which eventually dies back. Remove injured or infected growth promptly and ventilate greenhouses, as plants under glass are particularly susceptible.

Halo blight

Dwarf French and runner beans are vulnerable to this bacterial disease. Small dark spots with a yellow halo develop on leaves, which then turn yellow and die, resulting in poor growth and harvests. The bacteria are spread by water splash, so remove infected leaves and water the compost rather than showering plants.

Potassium deficiency

Commonly a problem where frequent watering washes potassium from the soil. Signs of deficiency are scorched, brown leaf tips and a purple tinge to foliage. Small flowers and poor fruit set are other symptoms. It can also lead to blotchy ripening on container-grown tomato plants. Apply a high-potash fertilizer such as tomato food.

Nitrogen deficiency

Small, yellowing leaves, occasionally with red and purple colouration, and lack of growth are symptoms of nitrogen deficiency. The oldest leaves tend to be affected first, but all parts of the plant will eventually look unwell. Apply nitrogen-rich fertilizers and replace or top up the compost in pots regularly.

Plant guide

The range of crops available to gardeners is vast and each one has numerous different cultivars, which can offer disease resistance, as well crops in an assortment of colours, flavours, shapes, and sizes. To help you choose, use this simple plant guide to select the best fruit and vegetables for your garden and your choice of containers. The symbols below indicate the conditions each crop requires.

Key to plant symbols
Soil preference

◌	Well-drained soil
◍	Moist soil
◌ ◍	Well drained or moist soil

Preference for sun or shade

☼	Full sun
☼	Partial or dappled shade
☼ ☼	Either full sun or partial shade

Hardiness ratings

✳✳✳	Fully hardy plants
✳✳	Plants that survive outside in mild regions or sheltered sites
✳	Plants that need protection from frost over winter

Tree fruits: apples and pears

Apple 'Ashmead's Kernel'
Aromatic and sweet, this old English russet dessert apple is prized for its excellent flavour, beautiful blossom, and ability to crop well in cooler climates. The fruit will keep until late winter if stored carefully.

Plant: late autumn to early spring
Harvest: mid-autumn

✽✽✽ ◐ ☼

Apple 'Golden Noble'
Large yellow fruits with a hint of sharpness, combined with good disease resistance, make this one of the most desirable cooking apple cultivars. Fruits sweeten on storage and keep well for up to two months.

Plant: late autumn to early spring
Harvest: mid-autumn

✽✽✽ ◐ ☼

Apple 'Royal Gala'
A familiar dessert apple from New Zealand, with red-flushed skin, pale yellow flesh and a mild flavour that is best when fruits are freshly picked. Partially self-fertile, it produces reliable crops year after year.

Plant: late autumn to early spring
Harvest: mid-autumn

✽✽✽ ◐ ☼

Apple 'Egremont Russet'
Heavy cropping and disease resistant, this delicious dessert apple is well suited to growing in a pot. The fruit is prized for its pale brown russet skin and dense, crisp, cream-coloured flesh with a rich, nutty flavour.

Plant: late autumn to early spring
Harvest: early to mid-autumn

✽✽✽ ◐ ☼

Apple 'Kidd's Orange Red'
Similar in flavour to 'Cox' but slightly sweeter and less prone to disease, this is a great dessert apple for the garden. Reliable crops of red-skinned, aromatic fruits keep their texture and flavour well when stored.

Plant: late autumn to early spring
Harvest: mid-autumn

✽✽✽ ◐ ☼

Apple 'Red Falstaff'
Heavy cropping, partially self-fertile and compact, 'Red Falstaff' is a good choice for a container. Crisp flesh with a good balance of sweetness and acidity makes this a refreshing dessert apple that is good for juicing.

Plant: late autumn to early spring
Harvest: mid-autumn

✽✽✽ ◐ ☼

Pear 'Williams' Bon Chrétien'
One of the most widely grown pear cultivars, thanks to its reliably heavy crop of pale green fruits with white juicy flesh. A delicious dessert or cooking pear, it has a deep, musky flavour and firm texture.

Plant: late autumn to early spring
Harvest: early autumn

❀❀❀ ◗ ☼

Pear 'Doyenne de Comice'
Widely considered one of the finest dessert pears, the large fruits are best stored after picking, and eaten a month or so later. A warm, sunny location will produce the best crop of sweet, russet-skinned fruits.

Plant: late autumn to early spring
Harvest: mid-autumn

❀❀❀ ◗ ☼

Pear 'Buerré Hardy'
This French dessert pear will bear the heaviest crops in a warm, sheltered spot. The good-sized fruits are best eaten soon after picking and have green, slightly russet skin and juicy, pale, perfumed flesh.

Plant: late autumn to early spring
Harvest: mid-autumn

❀❀❀ ◗ ☼

Pear 'Buerré Superfin'
A pear for the connoisseur, the round fruits have tender, yellow, sweet, scented flesh and are delicious raw or cooked. This cultivar needs a warm, sunny, sheltered spot if it is to produce reliable yields.

Plant: late autumn to early spring
Harvest: early autumn

❀❀❀ ◗ ☼

Pear 'Clapp's Favourite'
Ideal as a dessert or cooking pear, this American cultivar is a particularly prolific cropper. The long, yellow, smooth-skinned fruits are flushed with red, have crisp yellow flesh, and are best eaten soon after picking.

Plant: late autumn to early spring
Harvest: late summer

❀❀❀ ◗ ☼

Pear 'Concorde'
Well suited to training as a cordon or espalier, this popular commercial cultivar is compact, heavy cropping and easy to grow. The large, juicy, tender fruits are delicious raw and store well for several months.

Plant: late autumn to early spring
Harvest: mid-autumn

❀❀❀ ◗ ☼

Tree fruits

Cherry 'Stella' A popular garden cultivar, this dessert cherry bears abundant harvests of large, sugary, dark red fruits. It is also self-fertile, which means plenty of cherries will set if it is grown alone, without another tree to pollinate it.

Plant: late autumn to early spring
Harvest: midsummer

✽✽✽ ◗ ☼

Cherry 'Morello'
'Morello' is the best-known acid cherry, and is ideal for cooking and bottling. It produces attractive crops of bright red fruits and is ideal where there is only space for a single tree because it is self-fertile (see 'Stella').

Plant: late autumn to early spring
Harvest: midsummer

✽✽✽ ◗ ☼

Apricot 'Flavorcot'
This apricot is a good choice for cooler climates as it is late flowering, making it less likely that frost will adversely affect fruit set. The large, pink-tinged apricots have a rich flavour and suit both dessert and culinary uses.

Plant: late autumn to early spring
Harvest: late summer

✽✽✽ ◗ ☼

Plum 'Opal'
An excellent early dessert plum with yellow fruits that are flushed purple when ripe. They have a sweet flavour with just a hint of sourness, similar to 'Victoria' plums. The flowers are also self-fertile, which ensures heavy crops.

Plant: late autumn to early spring
Harvest: late summer

✽✽✽ ◗ ☼

Plum 'Victoria'
This popular pink-blushed plum has a firm texture and delicious sweet flavour when eaten raw or cooked. It is self-fertile, which means you only need one tree to produce a bumper crop of the attractive fruits.

Plant: late autumn to early spring
Harvest: late summer

✽✽✽ ◗ ☼

Peach 'Avalon Pride'
Peaches grow well in cooler climates, but their early blossom is often damaged by frosts, so grow under glass or protect with fleece. 'Avalon Pride' is a new American cultivar with resistance to peach leaf curl.

Plant: late autumn to early spring
Harvest: summer to early autumn

✽✽✽ ◗ ☼

Nectarine 'Fantasia'

Vigorous and reliable, this self-fertile tree will produce a good crop in cooler climates if given a warm, sunny site. The medium-sized fruits have striking deep red skins and juicy yellow flesh with a sweet flavour.

Plant: late autumn to early spring
Harvest: late summer

❄❄❄ ◊ ☼

Fig 'Brunswick'

Large, hand-shaped leaves and pretty purple-stained fruits make this an attractive plant to train against a south-facing wall. Bred for cooler conditions, this cultivar reliably produces mid-sized, pink-fleshed figs.

Plant: late autumn to early spring
Harvest: late summer

❄❄❄ ◊ ☼

Calamondin

A popular ornamental plant, this dwarf tree produces small, round, orange fruits. When ripe their flesh is sweet with an acidic note, and they are best used for marmalades and drinks, rather than eaten raw.

Plant: early to mid-spring
Harvest: year-round

❄ ◊ ☼

Kumquat

Closely related to other citrus fruits, but not a member of the *Citrus* genus, the kumquat is more tolerant of cold, being hardy down to -5°C (23°F). The small, oval, pleasantly bitter fruits are eaten whole.

Plant: early to mid-spring
Harvest: year-round

❄❄ ◊ ☼

Lemon 'Meyer'

This attractive evergreen is fast growing and produces scented white flowers and fruits throughout the year, making it a good choice for beginners. The fruits are thin-skinned and ideal for cooking.

Plant: early to mid-spring
Harvest: year-round

❄ ◊ ☼

Orange 'Valencia'

Worth growing if only for the delectable orange blossom scent that will fill the air on your patio or in a conservatory. These handsome trees also produce juicy, sweet oranges when given reliably high temperatures.

Plant: early to mid-spring
Harvest: winter

❄ ◊ ☼

Soft fruits

Strawberry 'Christine'

An early cropping cultivar, with large, juicy fruits, 'Christine' is ideal for growing in pots. It has also been bred with good resistance to the common diseases – verticillium wilt and powdery mildew – that attack plants.

Plant: summer
Harvest: early summer

❄❄❄ ◊ ☼

Strawberry 'Lucy'

A new mid-season cultivar that reliably produces excellent yields of deep red, glossy, sugary fruit. It has been bred to tolerate wet summer conditions, which cause many other strawberries to rot or fail to ripen.

Plant: summer
Harvest: early to midsummer

❄❄❄ ◊ ☼

Strawberry 'Elegance'

Well suited to growing in pots, this mid-season strawberry bears bumper crops of large, healthy, sweet fruits throughout the summer. It also shows useful resistance to verticillium wilt and powdery mildew.

Plant: summer
Harvest: early to midsummer

❄❄❄ ◊ ☼

Strawberry Malling Pearl

Plant ever-bearing strawberries, such as Malling Pearl, in spring and they will produce a steady supply of fruits from summer to autumn. This variety bears red, conical fruits with firm, juicy flesh and a sweet flavour.

Plant: spring
Harvest: midsummer to autumn

❄❄❄ ◊ ☼

Alpine strawberry

These tough little plants produce small fruits all summer, with a more subtle flavour than larger strawberries. Plants are easy to grow from seed sown in spring or from runners in summer, and will crop year after year.

Sow: spring **Plant**: midsummer
Harvest: summer

❄❄❄ ◊ ☼ ☀

Blackberry 'Ouachita'

A relatively new thornless blackberry with attractive erect canes that are easy to train, 'Ouachita' produces high yields of large, sweet, dark berries each summer. This cultivar is also resistant to disease.

Plant: late autumn to early spring
Harvest: midsummer

❄❄❄ ◊ ☼ ☀

Blackberry 'Black Satin'
One of the first thornless blackberries to fruit, the pretty pink flowers are followed by heavy crops of glossy, deep purple-black fruits. For the best flavour plant it in a large container in a sunny position.

Plant: late autumn to early spring
Harvest: mid- to late summer

❀❀❀ ◐ ☼ ☀

Blackberry 'Navaho'
This late-cropping blackberry cultivar, bred in the USA, produces clusters of huge, sugary-sweet berries. The thornless canes make it ideal for pots and the fruits are easy to pick.

Plant: late autumn to early spring
Harvest: late summer to early autumn

❀❀❀ ◐ ☼ ☀

Blackberry 'Loch Ness'
Compact and thornless, this blackberry is easy to manage where space is limited. The berries are larger than most, ripen to a lovely dark colour and have a sweet flavour.

Plant: late autumn to early spring
Harvest: late summer to early autumn

❀❀❀ ◐ ☼ ☀

Blackberry 'Waldo'
An excellent compact, thornless blackberry, ideal for growing in large containers in small gardens. This American early season cultivar produces a generous crop of long, sweet, full-flavoured berries.

Plant: late autumn to early spring
Harvest: midsummer

❀❀❀ ◐ ☼ ☀

Gooseberry 'Hinnomaki Red'
Used as a culinary gooseberry, but often sweet enough to eat fresh, these unusual red fruits have a delicious aromatic flavour. The neat bushes also offer good resistance to American gooseberry mildew.

Plant: late autumn to early spring
Harvest: early to midsummer

❀❀❀ ◐ ☼ ☀

Gooseberry 'Invicta'
Popular thanks to its resistance to American gooseberry mildew and bumper crops of large, pale green berries, the tasty fruit of 'Invicta' is often too tart to eat raw but makes great jams, chutneys, and crumbles.

Plant: late autumn to early spring
Harvest: early summer

❀❀❀ ◐ ☼ ☀

Soft fruits *continued*

Blueberry 'Bluetta'

Ideal for cooler climates because it blooms later than other cultivars, reducing the chance of frost damage, yet still ripens early, producing good yields of sweet fruits. The plants are compact and have red autumn leaves.

Plant: late autumn to early spring
Harvest: midsummer

❋❋❋ ◌ ☼

Blueberry 'Jersey'

This popular, late-cropping blueberry is easy to grow and tolerant of a range of soils. The abundant berries are quite small but sweet, making them perfect for cooking.

Plant: late autumn to early spring
Harvest: late summer to early autumn

❋❋❋ ◌ ☼

Blueberry 'Berkeley'

A good choice for a sheltered spot, but this blueberry will not crop well in cool regions. The juicy berries are produced quite late and bushes also sport bright yellow stems that look good in winter.

Plant: late autumn to early spring
Harvest: late summer

❋❋❋ ◌ ☼

Blueberry 'Coville'

For several weeks during the summer, clusters of large, purple-blue berries weigh down the branches of this upright, mid-season blueberry. The fruits have excellent flavour and keep particularly well in the fridge.

Plant: late autumn to early spring
Harvest: mid- to late summer

❋❋❋ ◌ ☼

Blueberry 'Spartan'

Early cropping and vigorous, this blueberry has large berries with a distinctive sweet, tangy flavour. It makes an attractive upright bush with large leaves that turn orange and yellow in autumn.

Plant: late autumn to early spring
Harvest: midsummer

❋❋❋ ◌ ☼

Blueberry 'Herbert'

Widely considered to be one of the tastiest blueberries, this cultivar bears heavy crops of extremely large, mid-blue berries on a vigorous bush. The plant's upright habit is ideal for pots in small gardens or on patios.

Plant: late autumn to early spring
Harvest: late summer

❋❋❋ ◌ ☼ ☽

Whitecurrant 'Blanka'
One of the most reliable and prolific whitecurrants, 'Blanka' produces an abundance of yellowish-white berries on long trusses that ripen in midsummer and are sweet enough to eat fresh or to make into preserves.

Plant: late autumn to early spring
Harvest: midsummer

✻✻✻ ◊ ☼

Redcurrant 'Red Lake'
A popular redcurrant prized for its generous crops of deliciously flavoured ruby-red fruits. Berries form on long strings that make them easy to pick, and they can be stored by freezing or making preserves.

Plant: late autumn to early spring
Harvest: midsummer

✻✻✻ ◊ ☼ ◐

Redcurrant 'Jonkheer van Tets'
One of the earliest redcurrants to crop in summer, this tough cultivar produces reliable yields of plump, juicy, glowing red fruits that look attractive hanging among the bright green foliage.

Plant: late autumn to early spring
Harvest: midsummer

✻✻✻ ◊ ☼ ◐

Redcurrant 'Rovada'
A late-cropping redcurrant with good resistance to disease, this cultivar bears abundant, large, jewel-like berries on long trusses that make picking quick and easy. Fruits have an excellent flavour, ideal for puddings.

Plant: late autumn to early spring
Harvest: mid- to late summer

✻✻✻ ◊ ☼ ◐

Blackcurrant 'Ben Sarek'
The compact nature of this cultivar makes it well suited to growing in pots. It also has good mildew resistance and produces an abundant crop of full-flavoured fruits, which are perfect for freezing or jam-making.

Plant: late autumn to early spring
Harvest: midsummer

✻✻✻ ◊ ☼

Blackcurrant 'Ben Lomond'
Late flowering allows this mid-season cultivar to set good crops in areas that suffer from late frosts. Heavy yields of large, tasty berries are borne on short strings, but plants can be susceptible to mildew.

Plant: late autumn to early spring
Harvest: midsummer

✻✻✻ ◊ ☼

Peas and beans

Pea 'Sugar Snap'
Either pick this versatile pea young and eat the whole pod, or leave it on the plant for longer to mature if you want fresh peas. Plants can grow up to 1.8m (6ft) tall, so they will need supports.

Sow: early spring to early summer
Harvest: late spring to late summer

❄❄ ◊ ◖ ☀

Pea 'Ambassador'
Compact vines make this robust pea ideal for growing in pots, and it bears lots of fat, blunt-ended pods packed with tender peas. Sow a batch of seeds every few weeks for a continuous crop.

Sow: early spring to early summer
Harvest: late spring to early autumn

❄❄ ◊ ◖ ☀

Peas 'Waverex'
Easy to grow and high yielding, this short-vined pea is a great choice for containers. The curved pods are produced in pairs and contain many tiny sugary peas that are delicious eaten raw and great for freezing.

Sow: early spring to early summer
Harvest: late spring to early autumn

❄❄ ◊ ◖ ☀

French Bean 'Goldfield'
Colourful and productive, 'Goldfield' yields good crops of unusual flat yellow beans. The tasty pods are tender and stringless, and make an interesting alternative to runner beans.

Sow: mid-spring to early summer
Harvest: early summer to early autumn

❄ ◊ ◖ ☀

French Bean 'Blue Lake'
In small gardens, grow this high-yielding bean up canes or trellis in large pots. Plants also cope well with dry conditions. Eat their stringless, sweet, green pods raw or cooked.

Sow: mid-spring to early summer
Harvest: early summer to mid-autumn

❄ ◊ ◖ ☀

Dwarf French Bean 'Purple Queen'
Perfect for pots, this compact bean needs no support and looks striking when laden with purple pods. The tasty, stringless beans freeze well and turn green when cooked.

Sow: mid-spring to early summer
Harvest: early summer to early autumn

❄ ◊ ◖ ☀

Dwarf French Bean 'Speedy'

Quick to crop, the young green pods of 'Speedy' can be ready to pick from the compact bushes in as little as seven weeks after sowing, making it perfect for beginners.

Sow: mid-spring to early summer
Harvest: early summer to early autumn

❄ ◌ ◑ ☼

Runner Bean 'White Lady'

A reliable runner bean, which sets good crops, even during hot weather, making it suitable for later sowings. The pure white flowers are not as attractive to birds as red blooms, making them less prone to damage.

Sow: mid-spring to early summer
Harvest: midsummer to mid-autumn

❄ ◌ ◑ ☼

Runner Bean 'Painted Lady'

Almost as good to look at as it is to eat, this bean has bold, bicoloured red and white flowers that are highly ornamental. It also produces good crops of delicious, long, tender beans but will need a large pot and supports.

Sow: mid-spring to early summer
Harvest: midsummer to mid-autumn

❄ ◌ ◑ ☼

Runner Bean 'Hestia'

This early-cropping, dwarf cultivar grows well in pots, needs no support, and is perfect for exposed gardens and balconies. The red and white flowers are followed by tasty, long, stringless beans that freeze well.

Sow: mid-spring to early summer
Harvest: midsummer to mid-autumn

❄ ◌ ◑ ☼

Runner Bean 'Enorma'

Popular for its straight and slender, stringless pods that can grow up to 50cm (20in) in length. Plant 'Enorma' in a large container and provide long, sturdy canes to support the heavily laden stems.

Sow: mid-spring to early summer
Harvest: midsummer to mid-autumn

❄ ◌ ◑ ☼

Runner Bean 'St George'

A new British-bred runner bean that has proved to be one of the heaviest cropping in trials. Striking bicoloured red and white flowers are followed by crisp, juicy, flavoursome beans over a long period.

Sow: mid-spring to early summer
Harvest: midsummer to mid-autumn

❄ ◌ ◑ ☼

Roots

Beetroot 'Red Ace'

Dark red, globe-shaped roots grow vigorously and uniformly, standing well in the soil without becoming woody. A good choice for pots because it withstands drier conditions.

Sow: early spring to midsummer
Harvest: early summer to mid-autumn

❋❋❋ ◊ ☼

Beetroot 'Burpee's Golden'

The bright yellow flesh of these roots make this easy-to-grow old variety a colourful curiosity. They have a sweet flavour and look striking when used raw in salads or cooked in pickles.

Sow: mid-spring to midsummer
Harvest: early summer to mid-autumn

❋❋❋ ◊ ☼

Beetroot 'Chioggia'

Both beautiful and delicious, this spherical root has rich red skin and white flesh stained with concentric rings of pink. Its mild, sweet, earthy flavour is good both raw and cooked.

Sow: mid-spring to midsummer
Harvest: early summer to mid-autumn

❋❋❋ ◊ ☼

Beetroot 'Moneta'

This cultivar produces a single plant from each seed, rather than several, reducing the need for thinning out. A good bolt-resistant choice for early sowings, it has tasty spherical roots.

Sow: early spring to early summer
Harvest: early summer to mid-autumn

❋❋❋ ◊ ☼

Beetroot 'Boltardy'

A trusty old favourite that reliably yields deep red, globe-shaped roots with a sweet flavour. One of the best for sowing under cloches in early spring due to its resistance to bolting.

Sow: early spring to midsummer
Harvest: early summer to mid-autumn

❋❋❋ ◊ ☼

Carrot 'Parmex'

One of the easiest carrots to grow in containers due to its squat, almost spherical roots, which don't require especially deep soil. They have a delicious sweet flavour and grow well from early sowings.

Sow: early spring to late spring
Harvest: late spring to early autumn

❋❋❋ ◊ ☼

Carrot 'Chantenay Red Cored'

Popular for its full flavour, small core and rich orange colour, the first sowings of this early maincrop carrot will be ready to harvest by the beginning of autumn. Its stumpy roots are also perfect for pots.

Sow: mid-spring to early summer
Harvest: early autumn to winter

❄❄❄ ◌ ☼

Carrot 'Rainbow'

True to their name these carrots come in an appealing mixture of creams, yellows, and oranges. A maincrop cultivar, the long, slender roots stand well in the soil in a deep container until you are ready to harvest.

Sow: mid-spring to early summer
Harvest: late summer to late autumn

❄❄❄ ◌ ☼

Carrot 'Carson'

This maincrop carrot takes longer to mature than early varieties, but has a denser texture and is perfect for autumn dishes. The medium-sized, tapering roots are rich orange and have a full, sweet flavour.

Sow: mid-spring to midsummer
Harvest: late summer to early winter

❄❄❄ ◌ ☼

Carrot 'Cosmic Purple'

The combination of smooth purple skins and bright orange cores make dramatic carrot slices, while the high sugar content means they taste good too. Cover early sowings with cloches or fleece to protect them from frost.

Sow: early spring to midsummer
Harvest: midsummer to late autumn

❄❄❄ ◌ ☼

Carrot 'Resistafly'

Resistance to attack by carrot fly makes this a useful cultivar in any garden. A maincrop carrot, the long, blunt-ended roots have a sweet flavour and dense texture that gives a satisfying crunch.

Sow: mid-spring to early summer
Harvest: late summer to late autumn

❄❄❄ ◌ ☼

Carrot 'Red Samurai'

Bred in Japan, this unusual summer-cropping carrot sports red skin and pink-tinged flesh that will brighten up any dish. The long, sweet roots will grow perfectly straight in deep pots.

Sow: early spring to early summer
Harvest: midsummer to early autumn

❄❄❄ ◌ ☼

Roots *continued*

Potato 'Nicola'

A reliable second early that produces heavy crops of long, yellow, waxy tubers that taste great boiled, roasted, or baked. It is also fairly resistant to potato blight, which is useful, especially in wetter regions.

Plant: mid-spring
Harvest: from midsummer

❄ ⬤ ◗ ☀

Potato 'Pink Fir Apple'

A fascinating old maincrop cultivar, producing long, irregular tubers with pink-flushed skin that is best left on during cooking. The waxy flesh, with its earthy flavour, makes this a popular salad potato.

Plant: mid-spring
Harvest: from early autumn

❄ ⬤ ◗ ☀

Potato 'Desiree'

Red-skinned, with tasty yellow, waxy flesh, this maincrop potato is particularly suitable for baking and mashing, but is a good all-rounder. It crops well, even in dry conditions, and is a good choice for containers.

Plant: mid-spring
Harvest: from early autumn

❄ ⬤ ◗ ☀

Potato 'Charlotte'

This supermarket favourite is deservedly popular, due to its smooth, yellow tubers and delicious waxy flesh. This second early grows well in containers and is one of the finest salad potatoes around.

Plant: mid-spring
Harvest: midsummer to late summer

❄ ⬤ ◗ ☀

Potato 'Congo' (minituber)

This heritage variety is available as disease-free minitubers with dark purple skins and startling blue flesh. A maincrop, it will produce a reasonable number of potatoes and plenty of interest at the table.

Plant: mid-spring
Harvest: from early autumn

❄ ⬤ ◗ ☀

Potato 'Kerr's Pink'

The blush-pink tubers have delicious cream, floury flesh, perfect for baking, mashing, chipping, and roasting. Versatile and high-yielding, this maincrop is a good choice for growing in pots. The tubers also store well.

Plant: mid-spring
Harvest: from early autumn

❄ ⬤ ◗ ☀

Potato 'Swift'

One of the fastest first early potatoes to crop, 'Swift' produces good yields of waxy, white tubers that make great salad potatoes. Plants also have short leaf and flower stems and are ideal for growing in windy situations.

Plant: early spring
Harvest: late spring to late summer

❄ ◌ ◍ ☼

Potato 'Yukon Gold'

The buttery, pale yellow flesh of this second early cultivar is great for baking, roasting, and mashing, making it an excellent choice if you have limited space. The golden-skinned tubers are also easy to peel.

Plant: mid-spring
Harvest: midsummer to late summer

❄ ◌ ◍ ☼

Radish 'French Breakfast'

Easy and quick to grow, this torpedo-shaped cultivar has rosy-red skin with a bright white tip. Its shape makes it perfect for slicing and the crisp flesh has a mild flavour with just a hint of peppery heat.

Sow: early spring to autumn
Harvest: mid-spring to autumn

❄❄ ◌ ◍ ☼ ☼

Radish 'Cherry Belle'

These spherical, bright red radishes tolerate dry soils and grow quickly, making them one of the best crops for beginners. The roots are best eaten small, but are slow to become woody, and have a mild flavour.

Sow: early spring to autumn
Harvest: mid-spring to autumn

❄❄ ◌ ◍ ☼ ☼

Radish 'Mantanghong'

Exotic, but simple to grow, this winter radish produces tennis ball-sized roots that stand well in the soil through cold weather. The pale green outer skin conceals vivid magenta-pink flesh which has a mild, nutty flavour.

Sow: early summer to midsummer
Harvest: late summer to winter

❄❄❄ ◌ ◍ ☼ ☼

Radish 'Saxa 2'

The bright pink-red skins and crisp, pure white flesh of 'Saxa 2' add colour and texture to salads. While it is quick to crop, the roots are slow to become tough, although, like all radishes, they are best harvested when young.

Sow: early spring to autumn
Harvest: mid-spring to autumn

❄❄ ◌ ◍ ☼ ☼

Stems and bulbs

Celeriac 'Monarch'

If sown inside in spring and kept well-watered once planted out, celeriac is not difficult to grow. This variety has a relatively smooth skin and creamy flesh which adds a delicate celery flavour to soups and stews.

Sow: early spring to mid-spring
Harvest: early autumn to winter

❄❄ ◗ ☼

Kohl rabi 'Purple Danube'

The vibrant purple stems and skin of this cultivar are highly ornamental and its sweet, nutty flavour is good raw or cooked. Purple types take longer to mature than white, so plant both for a longer cropping season.

Sow: early spring to late summer
Harvest: early summer to autumn

❄❄ ◌ ☼

Shallot 'Pikant'

An excellent old cultivar, usually grown from sets, this shallot crops heavily, has a strong flavour and keeps well after harvest. It is also one of the best for early planting due to its resistance to bolting.

Plant: early spring
Harvest: midsummer to early autumn

❄❄❄ ◌ ☼

Leek 'Musselburgh'

Reliable and hardy, this sturdy leek produces broad white stems with a sweet flavour when cooked. Try planting them close together in pots for even sweeter baby leeks.

Sow: early spring to mid-spring
Plant: late spring to early summer
Harvest: late autumn to late winter

❄❄❄ ◌ ☼

Leek 'Titan'

This winter stalwart stands through the coldest weather and makes warming soups and stews. Earth-up during growth in a deep pot for long, thick stems with a good flavour.

Sow: early spring to mid-spring
Plant: late spring to early summer
Harvest: late autumn to late winter

❄❄❄ ◌ ☼

Onion 'Purplette'

Versatile and delicious, this purple-skinned onion can be picked when young and juicy for pretty salad onions or left to produce small mature bulbs, perfect for pickling.

Sow: early spring to midsummer
Harvest: early summer to early autumn

❄❄❄ ◌ ☼

Onion 'Red Brunswick'

These large, red-skinned onions look as decorative growing in pots as they do sliced in salads. They can be picked when young in summer or left for the skins to mature before storing.

Sow: early spring to mid-spring
Harvest: late summer to early autumn

❄❄❄ ◌ ☼

Spring Onion 'White Lisbon'

A trusted old favourite, the white bulbs and bright green tops of this cultivar have a good, strong flavour. It is easy to grow, but prone to downy mildew, so thin plants to avoid the spread of disease.

Sow: early spring to late summer
Harvest: late spring to autumn

❄❄❄ ◌ ☼

Spring Onion 'Guardsman'

Long, straight, white stems make this a particularly attractive salad onion. It is tough, easy to grow and matures quickly; sow seeds fortnightly during the growing season for a continuous crop until the end of autumn.

Sow: early spring to late summer
Harvest: late spring to autumn

❄❄❄ ◌ ☼

Florence Fennel

The pure white bulbs of Florence fennel have a sweet, aniseed flavour and the feathery foliage is also attractive. Choose a cultivar with good resistance to bolting. Keep well watered so bulbs reach a good size.

Sow: mid-spring to early summer
Harvest: early summer to autumn

❄❄ ◌ ◑ ☼

Garlic

Garlic is easy to grow from cloves pushed into the compost in a large pot. Try the cultivar 'Solent Wight' for cooler climates or giant 'Elephant Garlic' (above) which produces bulbs up to 10cm (4in) in diameter.

Plant: Late autumn and late winter
Harvest: midsummer to late summer

❄❄❄ ◌ ☼

Rhubarb

Easy to grow in a large container if kept well fed and watered. The old cultivar 'Champagne' (above) is early cropping and ideal for forcing, while 'Giant Grooveless Crimson' is relatively compact and not too acidic.

Plant: early spring or autumn
Harvest: late winter to mid-spring

❄❄❄ ◌ ◑ ☼ ☼

Leafy vegetables

Kale 'Redbor'
The burgundy, ruffled leaves of this kale look wonderful right through winter and can be harvested during the coldest months. Easy to grow, it can also be cropped early when the young leaves are tender.

Sow: early spring to early summer
Harvest: early winter to mid-spring

❄❄❄ ◌ ◗ ☼ ☀

Kale 'Nero di Toscana'
Also known as 'Black Tuscan' or 'Cavolo Nero', this is the kale Italians favour for its elegant appearance and rich flavour. The slim, upright leaves are dark green and blistered like a Savoy cabbage.

Sow: early spring to early summer
Harvest: early winter to mid-spring

❄❄❄ ◌ ◗ ☼ ☀

Lettuce 'Little Gem'
A familiar supermarket form, but tastier when freshly picked, this miniature cos lettuce is crisp, sweet and quick to crop. Its small size makes it ideal for growing in containers and raised beds.

Sow: early spring to midsummer
Harvest: late spring to early autumn

❄ ◌ ◗ ☼ ☀

Lettuce 'Mottistone'
Unusual and highly ornamental, this hearting lettuce has fresh green, wavy leaves flecked with deep red. Combine it with flowers or other vegetables to make a pretty container display until it's ready to harvest.

Sow: early spring to midsummer
Harvest: late spring to early autumn

❄ ◌ ◗ ☼ ☀

Lettuce 'Lollo Rossa'
The red-edged, frilly leaves of this lettuce add colour and texture to salads and interest to productive pots. A loose-leaf cultivar, leaves can be picked as required or the whole head cut at once.

Sow: early spring to midsummer
Harvest: late spring to early autumn

❄ ◌ ◗ ☼ ☀

Lettuce 'Winter Density'
A miniature cos lettuce, similar to 'Little Gem', this cultivar has dark green hearts and a full sweet flavour. It is hardy enough for late sowings and will crop in early spring if protected with a cloche over winter.

Sow: early spring to early autumn
Harvest: early spring to late autumn

❄❄ ◌ ◗ ☼ ☀

Corn salad (syn. Lamb's lettuce)
Rosettes of small, mild-flavoured leaves make a valuable addition to salads for most of the year. The plants tolerate a range of conditions and are tough enough to provide leaves to pick through the cold winter months.

Sow: early spring to late summer
Harvest: late spring to winter

❄❄❄ ◌ ◐ ☼ ☀

Radicchio
This red chicory has crisp, glossy, slightly bitter leaves that add interest to summer and autumn salads. The pretty plants form tight hearts at their centres and develop the deepest colour in cooler weather.

Sow: late spring to late summer
Harvest: early summer to late autumn

❄❄ ◌ ◐ ☼ ☀

Oriental mustard greens
Ruby-laced leaves and a strong peppery flavour make these leaves essential for salads and stir-fries. Spring and early summer sowings bolt quickly, so are best cut when young; later crops can be left to mature.

Sow: mid-spring to autumn
Harvest: late spring to late autumn

❄❄ ◌ ☼

Summer purslane
A tender, heat-loving plant, summer purslane has small, succulent leaves that make a refreshing addition to salads. Green- and yellow-leaved types are available and grow well in pots, but need shelter from wind.

Sow: late spring to early summer
Harvest: early to late summer

❄ ◌ ☼

Land cress
Ideal for shady spots not suited to other vegetables, land cress is a hardy crop that can be harvested during winter. The handsome, shiny, deep green leaves have a peppery taste similar to watercress.

Sow: late spring to autumn
Harvest: early summer to winter

❄❄❄ ◐ ☀

Chop suey greens
A great container crop, this is a form of chrysanthemum, grown for its aromatic, feathery leaves, which can be enjoyed raw in salads, steamed, or stir-fried. Easy to grow, plants crop over a long season.

Sow: early spring to late summer
Harvest: late spring to autumn

❄❄ ◌ ◐ ☼ ☀

Leafy vegetables and microgreens

Mizuna
Large plants of jagged-edged leaves with a delicate mustard flavour are easy to grow from summer sowings, and are delicious in stir-fries. Spring sowings tend to bolt, so are better cropped as baby leaves for salads.

Sow: late spring to autumn
Harvest: midsummer to winter

❋❋ ◊ ◑ ☼ ☀

Salad rocket
Easy and quick to grow, with an irresistible buttery, spicy flavour, this is a great crop for beginners. Sow successionally for a continuous supply and keep well watered, as plants run to seed rapidly in dry conditions.

Sow: early spring to autumn
Harvest: late spring to winter

❋❋❋ ◊ ☼ ☀

Wild rocket
A tough, perennial plant that produces slim, indented leaves with a strong peppery taste that packs a punch in salads. Will often overwinter with no protection, but can become bitter in dry soil.

Sow: early spring to late summer
Harvest: late spring to winter

❋❋❋ ◊ ☼ ☀

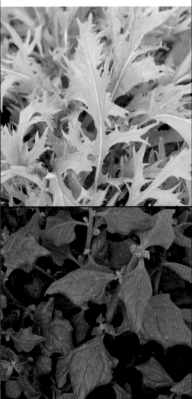

New Zealand spinach
This tender summer crop, with unusual, pointed, deep green foliage, is tolerant of dry conditions and stays looking good in intense sun where other leaf vegetables may wilt. It has a mild spinach-like taste.

Sow: late spring
Harvest: early to late summer

❋ ◊ ☼

Pak Choi
Essential for stir-fries and steaming, these elegant plants carry glossy, spoon-shaped leaves on thick, juicy stems. It is prone to bolting from early sowings, so unless baby leaves are required, sow throughout summer.

Sow: early to late summer
Harvest: late summer to autumn

❋ ◊ ◑ ☼ ☀

Chard 'Lucullus'
Decorative and delicious, this chard rapidly produces generous crops of big, shiny leaves on sturdy, white stems. Larger leaves can be boiled, steamed, or stir-fried, while baby leaves look good in salads.

Sow: early spring to late summer
Harvest: all year round

❋❋❋ ◊ ◑ ☼ ☀

Chard 'Bright Yellow'
The vibrant yellow stems of this chard will add a bold splash of colour to a container display. Sown in late summer, these sturdy plants will stand a mild winter and go on to produce a welcome early spring crop.

Sow: early spring to late summer
Harvest: all year round

Endive
Flat heads of frizzy, crisp, bright green leaves make an attractive display in containers and a choice late salad crop. They can be blanched by excluding light before harvesting to produce paler, sweeter leaves.

Sow: late spring to early summer
Harvest: late summer to autumn

Chicory 'Red Rib'
Closely related to the dandelion, this chicory is not fussy about its growing conditions and reliably produces an abundance of slightly bitter leaves with pretty red midribs that add a decorative touch to salads.

Sow: mid-spring to late summer
Harvest: early summer to autumn

Chicory 'Witloof'
Grow the long parsnip-like roots of this chicory through the summer and autumn and then force them in the dark in winter. This produces tight, pointed heads of pale leaves, known as 'chicons', to add to winter salads.

Sow: late spring to early summer
Harvest: winter

Microgreen Basil 'Dark Opal'
Quick and easy to grow as microgreens indoors, this purple-leaved basil also has purple-tinted stems and an intense, sweet aniseed flavour. It is a fashionable garnish for pasta dishes and salads.

Sow: all year round
Harvest: all year round

Microgreen Rocket 'Victoria'
Tiny salad rocket leaves have a mild peppery taste that adds a contemporary twist to salads and sandwiches. This microgreen is simple to grow at any time of year indoors and needs very little space.

Sow: all year round
Harvest: all year round

Fruiting vegetables

Aubergine 'Black Beauty'

A prolific cultivar, producing many shiny, deep purple, oval-shaped fruits. Like all aubergines, grow in full sun or, for the best yields, in a greenhouse or on a windowsill. Plants need supports.

Sow: early spring to late spring
Harvest: midsummer to early autumn

❄ ◌ ☼

Aubergine 'Bonica'

Plump, dark purple fruits are borne in profusion on these compact plants, which are ideal for growing in pots. Fruit sets easily and ripens early in a greenhouse on this excellent cultivar.

Sow: early spring to late spring
Harvest: midsummer to early autumn

❄ ◌ ☼

Aubergine 'Melanzana Viserba'

The unusual, long, almost black-skinned fruits are both decorative and delicious. This cultivar also crops well throughout summer in a greenhouse or sheltered site outdoors.

Sow: early spring to late spring
Harvest: midsummer to early autumn

❄ ◌ ☼

Aubergine 'Rosa Bianca'

A real gourmet aubergine, 'Rosa Bianca' has fat, egg-shaped fruits with lilac skins, and is a great specimen plant for a pot in a greenhouse or on a windowsill.

Sow: early spring to late spring
Harvest: midsummer to early autumn

❄ ◌ ☼

Courgette 'Black Forest'

Perfect where space is limited, this climbing courgette thrives in large pots and can be trained up a fence, trellis, or sturdy canes. It produces a heavy crop of dark green fruits.

Sow: mid-spring to early summer
Harvest: early summer to early autumn

❄ ◌ ☼

Courgette 'Jemmer'

An abundance of vibrant yellow fruits make this an attractive cultivar for a pot. The courgettes stand out among the leaves, and therefore are less likely to be missed and grow into marrows.

Sow: mid-spring to early summer
Harvest: early summer to early autumn

❄ ◌ ☼

Courgette 'Parador'
This golden-fruited cultivar matures early and will crop prolifically throughout summer if the courgettes are picked regularly while small and sweet. A striking variety for a pot.

Sow: mid-spring to early summer
Harvest: early summer to early autumn

❄ ◊ ☼

Courgette 'Zucchini'
Reliable and high yielding, this early cultivar can mature two weeks before standard crops. Its compact, bushy habit is ideal for pots and the dark-skinned fruits have a smooth texture.

Sow: mid-spring to early summer
Harvest: early summer to early autumn

❄ ◊ ☼

Courgette 'Eight Ball'
For something different try this compact courgette with its round, dark green fruits. Like all courgettes they are sweetest when picked small – the size of a cricket ball is ideal.

Sow: mid-spring to early summer
Harvest: early summer to early autumn

❄ ◊ ☼

Cucumber 'Marketmore'
A high-yielding cucumber that grows well outside when trained up trellis or a wigwam. This cultivar produces sturdy, deep green fruits up to 20cm (8in) long, and is resistant to viruses.

Sow: mid-spring to early summer
Harvest: early summer to early autumn

❄ ◊ ☼

Cucumber 'La Diva'
Easy to grow and prolific, this cucumber thrives in a greenhouse or warm spot outdoors and will produce a continuous supply of sweet, juicy, mini cucumbers throughout summer.

Sow: early spring to early summer
Harvest: early summer to early autumn

❄ ◊ ☼

Cucumber 'Crystal Apple'
The round, pale yellow-skinned, slightly spiny fruits are a bit of a novelty, and are sweet and juicy to eat. Train plants up supports in a warm area outdoors.

Sow: mid-spring to early summer
Harvest: early summer to early autumn

❄ ◊ ☼

Fruiting vegetables *continued*

Cucumber 'Cucino'
Best grown in a greenhouse or indoors by a south-facing window, this cucumber can also be grown outdoors in mild areas. It produces a heavy crop of juicy baby fruits.

Sow: early spring to early summer
Harvest: early summer to early autumn

❄ ◊ ☼

Cucumber 'Bella'
This greenhouse variety grows vigorously and yields many smooth, dark green, standard-size cucumbers. It produces sweet fruits, and is resistant to powdery mildew.

Sow: early spring to early summer
Harvest: early summer to early autumn

❄ ◊ ☼

Cucumber 'Gherkin'
Fast-growing and high-yielding, this cucumber is best grown up supports in a sunny spot outdoors. The small, pale, slightly prickly fruits are ideal for pickling, but can also be eaten raw.

Sow: mid-spring to early summer
Harvest: early summer to early autumn

❄ ◊ ☼

Pepper 'Mini Bell'
Decorative and perfect for patio containers, this compact plant produces an early crop of boxy sweet peppers that ripen from orange, through red, to chocolate brown.

Sow: early spring to mid-spring
Harvest: midsummer to early autumn

❄ ◊ ☼

Pepper 'Mohawk'
A dwarf habit makes this sweet pepper perfect for growing in a pot. It looks especially attractive when the fruits ripen to bright yellow. Can be grown outdoors in mild areas.

Sow: early spring to mid-spring
Harvest: midsummer to early autumn

❄ ◊ ☼

Pepper 'Gypsy'
This early sweet pepper yields good crops of thin-skinned fruits, which ripen from greenish-yellow to red. The fruits grow up to 10cm (4in) long and are great for salads or roasting.

Sow: early spring to mid-spring
Harvest: midsummer to early autumn

❄ ◊ ☼

Pepper 'Alma Paprika'
The fascinating squat fruits of this chilli pepper mature from pale cream through to red. They have a mild heat and sweet flavour, and can be eaten raw, cooked, or dried for storing.

Sow: early spring to mid-spring
Harvest: midsummer to early autumn

❄ ◊ ☀

Pepper 'Aji Amarillo'
A South American favourite, the long, pointed fruits ripen to yellow. They are medium hot and ideal for sauces and salsas. Like most chillies, they are best grown in a greenhouse or indoors.

Sow: early spring to mid-spring
Harvest: midsummer to early autumn

❄ ◊ ☀

Pepper 'Cherry Bomb'
Bright red, round chillies hang like baubles from these tall plants. The fruits are thick-skinned, medium hot and add a good chilli kick to salsas and cooked dishes.

Sow: early spring to mid-spring
Harvest: midsummer to early autumn

❄ ◊ ☀

Pepper 'Hungarian Hot Wax'
An attractive, bushy chilli pepper that bears tapering fruits which are sweet and yellow when young, becoming hot and red when mature. Grow in a greenhouse or on a sunny windowsill.

Sow: early spring to mid-spring
Harvest: midsummer to early autumn

❄ ◊ ☀

Summer Squash 'Sunburst'
Closely related to courgettes and used in exactly the same way, these bright yellow, flying saucer-shaped fruits look decorative when grown in pots and raised beds.

Sow: mid-spring to early summer
Harvest: early summer to early autumn

❄ ◊ ☀

Summer Squash 'Custard White'
Peculiar pale green fruits with scalloped edges are delicious when picked young and roasted or eaten raw. Like courgettes, they are easy to grow and yield heavy crops.

Sow: mid-spring to early summer
Harvest: early summer to early autumn

❄ ◊ ☀

Fruiting vegetables *continued*

Summer Squash 'Little Gem Rolet'

Round, yellow-fleshed fruits with dark green skins are produced in good numbers on this climbing plant. Train it up sturdy canes or trellis. The fruits have excellent flavour and store well.

Sow: mid-spring to early summer
Harvest: early summer to early autumn

❄ ◊ ☼

Winter Squash 'Sweet Dumpling'

Ideal for a small space, this vigorous plant needs support but is not as sprawling as some. The small, dark green fruits have decorative cream stripes and tasty pale flesh.

Sow: mid-spring to early summer
Harvest: late summer to mid-autumn

❄ ◊ ☼

Winter Squash 'Uchiki Kuri'

This fast-growing plant needs a large pot and plenty of fertilizer and water, but the rewards are large orange-skinned fruits, prized for their nutty, orange flesh. They also store well.

Sow: mid-spring to early summer
Harvest: late summer to mid-autumn

❄ ◊ ☼

Tomato 'Marmande'

A beefsteak tomato, the large, puckered, fleshy fruits have an intense flavour when ripe. They need constant heat to ripen, so grow in a greenhouse or outdoors in warm areas.

Sow: early spring to mid-spring
Harvest: late summer to mid-autumn

❄ ◊ ☼

Tomato 'Sungold'

This highly popular cherry tomato produces long trusses of small, orange, incredibly sweet fruits. It is a cordon variety, so needs staking and side-shooting to crop well, whether grown outdoors or under cover.

Sow: early spring to mid-spring
Harvest: midsummer to mid-autumn

❄ ◊ ☼

Tomato 'Tigerella'

Flavoursome red fruits streaked with yellow and green marks out this distinctive cultivar. The tomatoes also mature early. A cordon variety, plants require support and grow well indoors or outside.

Sow: early spring to mid-spring
Harvest: midsummer to mid-autumn

❄ ◊ ☼

Tomato 'Country Taste'
Best grown under glass, this beefsteak tomato produces huge, dense-fleshed fruits that are full-flavoured and perfect for slicing. Its cordon habit makes staking essential.

Sow: early spring to mid-spring
Harvest: late summer to mid-autumn

❄ ◌ ☼

Tomato 'Black Krim'
An heirloom cultivar with large, meaty fruits that turn red with an attractive hint of purple when ripe. They have a delicious sweet flavour and ripen early. Best supported and grown as a cordon.

Sow: early spring to mid-spring
Harvest: midsummer to mid-autumn

❄ ◌ ☼

Tomato 'Black Cherry'
A good choice for growing outdoors, this cherry tomato produces a heavy yield of sweet, juicy fruits that ripen to purple-tinged red. The tall, cordon plants need training up canes. It will also grow well under cover.

Sow: early spring to mid-spring
Harvest: midsummer to mid-autumn

❄ ◌ ☼

Tomato 'Tumbler'
This bush tomato will trail attractively over the sides of pots and hanging baskets and needs no staking. Plants produce prolific crops of small, red, cherry fruits that taste delicious, adding to this cultivar's appeal.

Sow: early spring to mid-spring
Harvest: midsummer to mid-autumn

❄ ◌ ☼

Sweetcorn
The tall, elegant plants need heat to produce a good crop and should be grown close together to aid pollination. Tendersweet cultivars, such as 'Lark', have the sweetest cobs.

Sow: mid-spring to early summer
Harvest: late summer to early autumn

❄ ◌ ☼

Baby Sweetcorn
These small cobs come from full-sized plants, but are picked when young, just as the silky tassels begin to show. They don't require pollinating, so don't need to be near other plants.

Sow: mid-spring to early summer
Harvest: early summer to late summer

❄ ◌ ☼

Herbs

Basil
The sweet, aniseed-flavoured leaves grow well from seed in a warm spot or on a windowsill. Try 'Sweet Genovese' (left) for the classic Italian herb, 'Purple Delight' (right) for dark leaves, or 'Siam Queen' for a stronger taste.

Sow: early spring to midsummer
Harvest: late spring to late autumn

❋ ◊ ☼

Chives
Easy to grow from seed or by splitting existing clumps in spring, this perennial herb produces grassy leaves with a mild onion flavour. Its pretty purple pompon flowers are a decorative bonus, and are also edible.

Sow: early to late spring
Harvest: early spring to late autumn

❋❋❋ ◊ ◑ ☼ ☀

Coriander
Essential for Asian cooking, coriander is easy to grow from seed. Sow in succession for a continuous supply, as it is prone to bolting. Choose a cultivar, such as 'Calypso', bred for the leaves rather than seeds.

Sow: early spring to late summer
Harvest: late spring to early autumn

❋❋❋ ◊ ☼ ☀

Fennel
Graceful and airy, fennel comes in green and bronze forms and may reach 1.8m (6ft) tall. A handsome perennial, its aniseed-flavoured, feathery leaves combine well with both flower and vegetable plantings.

Sow: early to late spring
Harvest: late spring to early autumn

❋❋❋ ◊ ☼

Mint
A refreshing perennial with a crisp, clean flavour, mint thrives in moist, shady conditions, which do not suit many other herbs, so keep pots well watered. It is also invasive and best planted on its own.

Plant: early spring to late spring
Harvest: late spring to early autumn

❋❋❋ ◊ ☀

Marjoram (syn. Oregano)
This herb will thrive in well-drained compost, and appears year after year. Easy to grow and to use in the kitchen, its rounded, yellow-green leaves and low, bushy habit make it ideal for pots or as a border edging.

Sow: mid-spring to early summer
Harvest: late spring to late autumn

❋❋❋ ◊ ☼ ☀

Curly-leaved Parsley

Masses of tightly curled, bright green, tasty leaves form handsome plants that stay green until winter weather sets in; plants then reappear in spring. Parsley dies after flowering in the second season, so sow every year.

Sow: early spring to late spring
Harvest: year-round

Flat-leaved Parsley

The Italian form of this classic herb is often preferred because it is easier to clean and chop. Easy to grow from seed, place it outside in summer and then bring inside to grow on a windowsill for leaves in winter.

Sow: early spring to late spring
Harvest: year-round

Rosemary

A narrow-leaved evergreen shrub, rosemary is at home in containers and provides welcome structure and winter interest. Its tough, highly aromatic leaves can be picked all year and it has pale blue spring flowers.

Plant: mid-spring to early summer
Harvest: year-round

Sage

Evergreen in all but the hardest winters, both the green and purple forms of this low-growing shrub have strongly scented, downy leaves. Easy to grow in pots, pinch out the shoot tips to keep plants bushy.

Plant: mid-spring to early summer
Harvest: year-round

Russian Tarragon

Hardy and easy to grow from seed, Russian tarragon has a milder, less refined aniseed flavour than the French type, but is more widely available. Plants grow quickly, so cut back regularly to keep them in check.

Sow: early spring to late summer
Harvest: late spring to autumn

Thyme

There are many types of thyme, with habits ranging from creeping to bushy, with various scents and flavours. They all grow well in free-draining compost and are clothed in small flowers in early summer.

Sow or plant: late spring
Harvest: year-round

Index

Index *continued*

Suppliers

Some of these suppliers are specialist nurseries and suppliers, so it is worth checking for opening hours before visiting; most also offer a mail order service.

Vegetable seeds & plants

Dobies of Devon
Tel: 0844 701 7625
www.dobies.co.uk
Seeds and young plants

Marshalls
Tel: 01480 443390
www.marshalls-seeds.co.uk
Seeds, young plants, fruit plants

Nicky's Nursery
01843 600972
www.nickys-nursery.co.uk
Vegetable seeds, with a comprehensive choice of chilli pepper seed

Pennard plants
01 749 860039
www.pennardplants.com
Heritage vegetable seeds and fruit plants

Pepperpot Nursery
01483 424614
www.pepperpotherbplants.co.uk
Specialist herb nursery

Simpson's Seeds
01985 845004
www.simpsonsseeds.co.uk
Wide range of vegetable seeds

Suttons Seeds
Tel: 0844 922 0606
www.suttons.co.uk
Seeds, young plants, and fruit bushes and trees

Thompson & Morgan
Tel: 0844 248 5383
www.thompson-morgan.com
Seeds, young plants, fruit trees and bushes

Fruit nurseries

Blackmoor Fruit Nursery
Tel: 01420 477978
www.blackmoor.co.uk
Fruit tree and bushes

Keepers Nursery
01622 726465
www.keepers-nursery.co.uk
Fruit trees

Ken Muir Ltd
Tel: 01255 830181
www.kenmuir.co.uk
Soft fruits and trees

Reads Nursery
01986 895 555
www.readsnursery.co.uk
Fruit trees and soft fruits

Victoriana Nursery Gardens
Tel: 01233 740529
www.victoriananursery.co.uk
Specialist fruit and vegetable nursery

Containers & equipment

Bells of Suffolk
01986 894456
www.bellsofsuffolk.com
Traditional and vintage planters and gardening tools

Burgon & Ball
0114 233 8262
www.burgonandball.com
High quality garden tools, planters and accessories

Crocus
Tel: 0844 557 2233
www.crocus.co.uk
Containers and growing bags

Harrod Horticultural (UK)
Tel: 0845 402 5300
www.harrodhorticultural.com
Tools, containers and growing bags

Joseph Bentley
01905 791984
www.josephbentley.co.uk
Traditional gardening tools

Plant Supports
01584 781578
www.plantsupports.co.uk
Large range of steel plant supports

Primrose London
Tel: 0118 945 9999
www.primrose.co.uk
Planters and containers

Sparrow and Finch
01892 861202
www.sparrowandfinch.co.uk
Contemporary high quality timber planters and growing tables

Spear and Jackson
Tel: 0114 281 4242
www.spear-and-jackson.com
High quality garden tools

The Terracotta Pot Company
Tel: 01964 501988
www.theterracottapotcompany.com
Frostproof terracotta containers

Whichford Pottery
Tel: 01608 684416
www.whichfordpottery.com
Hand-thrown frostproof terracotta pots and containers

Urbis Design
Tel: 01759 373839
www.urbisdesign.co.uk
Contemporary planters and pots

Acknowledgements

The publisher would like to thank the following for their kind permission to reproduce their photographs:

(Key: a-above; b-below/bottom; c-centre; f-far; l-left; r-right; t-top)

4 Dorling Kindersley: Airedale (tr, br). **9** GAP Photos: Friedrich Strauss (tr). The Garden Collection: Nicola Stocken Tomkins (crb). **10** GAP Photos: J S Sira (fcr). **11** Marianne Majerus Garden Images: MMGI (bc). **12-13** Marianne Majerus Garden Images: MMGI (ca). **13** GAP Photos: Friedrich Strauss (bl, br). **14** Marianne Majerus Garden Images: MMGI / Bennet Smith (tr). **20** Victoriana Nursery Gardens/Stephen Shirley: (cra). **22** GAP Photos: Friedrich Strauss (bl). **25** GAP Photos: Paul Debois (br). **27** GAP Photos: Janet Johnson (tr). **28** GAP Photos: Lee Avison (br); Friedrich Strauss (bc). **32-33** GAP Photos: Michael Howes (c). **44** Photolibrary: Gavin Kingcome (br). **46** GAP Photos: Graham Strong (bl). **47** Suttons Seeds: (br). **52** GAP Photos: Jonathan Buckley (tr). **53** Dorling Kindersley: Vanessa Hamilton (tr). **54** GAP Photos: Maxine Adcock (br). **55** Dorling Kindersley: Vanessa Hamilton (tl). **63** Dorling Kindersley: Alan Buckingham (tr). **64** Dorling Kindersley: Alan Buckingham (bl, bc, br). **65** GAP Photos: Paul Debois (br). **80** Dorling Kindersley: Airedale (tl). Amanda Jensen: (br). **82** Dorling Kindersley: Vanessa hamilton (br). **103** Alamy Images: blickwinkel (bl). Dorling Kindersley: Kim Taylor (cra). FLPA: Nigel Cattlin (br). **104** GAP Photos: Dave Bevan (cla). **105** Corbis: Peter Reynolds / Frank Lane Picture Agency (ca). GAP Photos: Dave Bevan (bl). Getty Images: Dea / L. Andena (cla). Royal Horticultural Society: (br). **107** GAP Photos: Dave Bevan (bl, cla). Royal Horticultural Society: (br); John Trenholm (cra). **108** FLPA: Nigel Cattlin (cla). GAP Photos: Dave Bevan (cra). Royal Horticultural Society: (br). Science Photo Library: Dr Jeremy Burgess (bc). **109** FLPA: Nigel Cattlin (br). Royal Horticultural Society: (cla, ca, bl). **112** Dorling Kindersley: Alan Buckingham (cla, cra). GAP Photos: Paul Debois (ca). **113** Dorling Kindersley: Alan Buckingham (cla, ca, cra, bl, br). Victoriana Nursery Gardens/ Stephen Shirley: (bc). **114** Dorling Kindersley: Alan Buckingham (cla, ca, cra, bl). **115** Dorling Kindersley: Alan Buckingham (ca). GAP Photos: Lee Avison (bl, cra); Friedrich Strauss (bc). Garden World Images: MAP / Frédéric Didillon (cla). Victoriana Nursery Gardens/Stephen Shirley: (br). **116** Dorling Kindersley: Alan Buckingham (cla, bl, br). **117** Dorling Kindersley: Alan Buckingham (ca, bl, br). Victoriana Nursery Gardens/Stephen Shirley: (cla). **118** Dorling Kindersley: Alan Buckingham (cla, ca, cra, bl, bc, br). **119** Dorling Kindersley: Alan Buckingham (ca, cra, bl). GAP Photos: Lee Avison (cla); Paul Debois (bc). Victoriana Nursery Gardens/Stephen Shirley: (br). **120** Suttons Seeds: (ca, br). Victoriana Nursery Gardens/Stephen Shirley: (cb). **121** GAP Photos: Lynn Keddie (ca). Suttons Seeds: (cla, cra, bl, br). **122** GAP Photos: Graham Strong (br). Suttons Seeds: (bl, bc). Victoriana Nursery Gardens/Stephen Shirley: (ca). **123** GAP Photos: Martin Hughes-Jones (br). Suttons Seeds: (cla, ca). Thompson & Morgan: (bc). Victoriana Nursery Gardens/Stephen Shirley: (bl). **124** Thompson & Morgan: (bc). **125** Marshalls Seeds: (cla). Suttons Seeds: (bc, br). **126** Marshalls Seeds: (bc, br). Suttons Seeds: (bl). **127** Dorling Kindersley: Airedale (bl). Marshalls Seeds: (cra). Thompson & Morgan: (ca). Victoriana Nursery Gardens/Stephen Shirley: (cla). **128** Marshalls Seeds: (cla, ca). **131** Photolibrary: Juliette Wade (cra). Suttons Seeds: (bl, bc, br). **132** The Cook's Garden: (bl). GAP Photos: Graham Strong (bc). Victoriana Nursery Gardens/Stephen Shirley: (cla, br). 133 Suttons Seeds: (bl). Victoriana Nursery Gardens/Stephen Shirley: (ca, cra, bc, br). **134** Dorling Kindersley: Airedale (br). Suttons Seeds: (ca). Thompson & Morgan: (bl, bc). Victoriana Nursery Gardens/Stephen Shirley: (cra). **135** Dorling Kindersley: Airedale (bc). GAP Photos: Jonathan Buckley (br). **136** Dorling Kindersley: Airedale (cla, ca, bl). Victoriana Nursery Gardens/Stephen Shirley: (bc). **137** Dorling Kindersley: Airedale (cra, bl). Victoriana Nursery Gardens/Stephen Shirley: (ca)

All other images © Dorling Kindersley
For further information see:
www.dkimages.com

Dorling Kindersley would also like to thank the following:

Index: **Jane Coulter**

Marshalls, **Suttons Seeds**, **Thompson & Morgan**, and **Victoriana Nursery Gardens** (see Suppliers list on p.143 for details) for the loan of images.

Suttons Seeds and **Thompson & Morgan** for supplying seeds and plants.

Harrod Horticultural (UK) for supplying containers and growing bags for photographic shoots (see Suppliers list on p.143 for details).